Alberto VENTUNO

ABSURDISTAN

The Diagnosis of a Sick Planet

*"In the sphere of thought, absurdity and perversity remain the masters of the world,
and their dominion is suspended only for brief periods. "*
Arthur Schopenhauer

"The privilege of absurdity; to which no living creature is subject, but man only. "
Thomas Hobbes

Foreword

Welcome to *Absurdistan*, a tiny dot in the middle of nowhere within a gigantic universe. The fallout of a cosmic accident in a cold and indifferent universe and home to a neurotic species called humans. Supposedly, we are a great vintage of the Universe and the result of a millenary fermentation, yet neither personally nor collectively we do not seem to have reached the maturity of a millennial civilization. At an individual level, life seems to have made us frustrated, dissatisfied and torn between suffering and boredom, and collectively we have never been so divided and mistrustful of each other. In addition, our complete disregard of the ecological balance of our planet has initiated the sixth mass extinction on Earth. Add to that socio-economic imbalances, wars, corruption, organized crime, and the gap between the rich and poor which continue to widen constantly.

Philosophically speaking, the human condition is well beyond tragic, it is *"absurd."* The term absurd is the antonym of logic, so considering the mathematical nature of the Universe how can it be absurd?

According to philosophers of absurd, the encounter between our tendency to seek inherent meaning in life and the silent answer of the universe, results in absurdity. Thus, the absurd is neither in us nor in the world, but in our common presence. Put differently, deprived of any rational or scientific answer as to the meaning of life, and by refusing the leap of faith, we are doomed to fall into absurdity.

This eternal tension between our desire for order, meaning and happiness and the universe's refusal to provide that, has made us all a bunch of neurotic and desperate souls trying to color life through compassion and striving for superhuman status. Indeed, you need to be a superman to embrace the struggle and the contradiction of living without purpose.

The French philosopher Albert Camus invites us to embark on a rebellion against the absurdity and according to him it is only through this courageous revolt that life becomes meaningful. It is all about living and doing it freely. Yet often this pursuit of escaping the absurd seems to be as futile as chasing our own tails. Nothing seems to be good enough for our perpetual quest of an elusive grand narrative about life. Maybe this very relentless hunger of ours for meaning is the reason for our suffering.

The only remaining option to overcome this existential dilemma is to view everything as significant, and to try to come up with our own answers in an irrational and meaningless universe. And this is the main purpose of this book, namely taking a look at absurdity in all its facets and trying to diagnose all the evils of humanity and provide some guidelines as how to put an end to our global mess. Let's take a journey into *Absurdistan*, a beautiful and twisted planet filled with a lot of paradoxes and contradictions and in desperate need to be straightened out. Would that put an end to our misery as a species?

The Cosmic Absurdity

Most probably 13.8 billion years ago, a highly dense peanut exploded and created our vast universe, measuring 100 billion light years in diameter. Yet, we have still no clue, why and how that happened. The same goes for the fate of the universe, where we still do not know whether it will continue to expand indefinitely, or at a certain point it would stop its expansion and begin contracting. In both cases we will be the losers and will eventually disappear completely, until a new universe is formed and even in that case what would be the chances of the same chain of events leading to life to happen again?

So, while the universe would never cease to exist, and the perpetual chain of Big Crunch and Big Bang would go on eternally, what is the point in all that waste of energy and material to create a cold and indifferent universe?

Moreover, when we rightfully question the point of existence, we are told by philosophers that we are asking the wrong question, namely by being part of the universe, we cannot get out of it and observe it and ask why it came around.

Another element of this cosmic absurdity is the fact that expansion of the Universe means that we live within a gigantic explosion. making everything impermanent and turning the Universe into a perennial inconsistence where two successive instants are never identical and where everything is constantly changing.

Faced with this relativism that surrounds us we get more desperate and squeeze our brains in search of truth, namely something deeper and more objective than a simple sensation. However, things get more absurd when we realize that truth is nothing more that correspondence between thought and reality, which means that our truth is not an objective reality but rather the representation that we make of it.

Living in a four-dimensional world, namely three spatial dimensions and one temporal one, we might be missing other possible dimensions that in turn would make us blind to the real nature of the universe. What if we were only Matrix-style biofuel for some superior beings?

In addition to this, living in the space-time continuum of the universe, we have our conception of time as the measure of the evolution of phenomena by attributing an order (present, past, and future) to events. However, knowing that space and time are intimately linked, the relativity of time amplifies the confusion that surrounds us.

After all everything we do is rooted in time and the world without time would stand still. Time, in classical terms, allows for the complete ordering of all events in the universe. Yet we are told by scientists that time is an illusion namely, that the feeling of time passing is only an impression created by the brain and the memory. In other words, the way in which our memory arranges our actions and the events that happen to us, creates the illusion of sequence, i.e., an impression of dynamism in a static world. As a result, our conceptions of a passed past and a coming future would be "emotional perceptions" and not a physical reality. Moreover, following the same logic, time would be neither independent nor unitary and has no global order. This means that time does not exist outside of us as an objective reality of nature. In such a scenario the past, present and future could coexist, which means that the world would be nothing but a vast collection of unrelated moments.

This fragilizes the foundation of temporality, i.e., the notions of past, present, and future and turns it into a human hallucination. Let's not forget that temporality governs almost everything: religion, language, thought and behavior.

Obviously, we should not expect anything logical to arise from this cosmic absurdity. The proof is our planet Earth which should rather be called

Absurdistan. A tiny, 4.5-billion-year-old planet which surprisingly enough has so far survived several cosmic events such as supernovae, quasars, violent solar flares, and multiple asteroid impacts. However, eventually, in a few billion years, it will be absorbed by the Sun which by then would have turned into a red giant.

In addition to all that Absurdistan created another cosmic surprise, namely life in an unanimated universe. Another cosmic accident leading to the chain of physics, chemistry, biochemistry, and biology, and consequently terrestrial life.

All we know is that life has begun in the depths of the liquid and chemically rich oceans, whereby some unknown mechanism, simple, anaerobic bacteria have emerged and have unwittingly transformed the Earth's carbon dioxide-rich atmosphere into one sufficiently oxygenated one to allow aerobic organisms to emerge and dominate the oceans and land. This led to biodiversity of the Earth, which was challenged 65 million years ago, when the Earth was hit by an asteroid that in turn wiped out more than 70% of the Earth's plant and animal species, including the dinosaurs that until then dominated other animal species. Thus, we were not supposed to be here, and it all happened by chance. Put differently, we are the fallouts of an "ecological tragedy" which came about by pure chance. The rest we know, we are descended from a big-brained branch of these mammals (primates) that evolved into Homo sapiens. This means that we are the result of a long and evolutionary process of life on Earth that makes us a species among other animal species. Yet thanks to our highly developed brain, we have managed to dominate other species. While sharing 98% of the genome of the chimpanzee, we consider ourselves the great vintage of universal fermentation and an empire within an empire.

This synthetic account of our universe makes us more confused than before. What on earth is the point of having a huge cold and silent universe with us left alone in the middle of nowhere?
What a waste of space and energy, a terrain of 100 billion light years just to create Absurdistan, a tiny planet and light its sky via more than 200 billion

stars, and then have it swallowed by the Sun its main source of life!

The Existential Absurdity

Cursed with consciousness and mortality, we are ill-equipped to endure the torment of our existential absurdity. We are thrown into existence and condemned to death without really knowing what we are accused of. Consequently, as a defensive mechanism, we tend to live as if we were not going to die. We prefer to forget our mortality because it enables us to look away from the fundamental absurdity of the human condition.

We avoid confrontation with the *absurd* by clinging onto *faith,* which gives us the answer that *reason* cannot give us. However, *reason* has no way of verifying the answer provided by the *faith.* Science can only say *how* and not *why.* Yet, faith is only a *bet,* a leap over the reason allowing us to fight the feeling of absurdity which could sink us into madness. Religion by providing a *"raison d'être (why)"* drugs us and helps us better bear the burden of existence. The price to pay, however, according to Danish philosopher Soren Kierkegaard would be a meta-rational leap beyond the reasonable: *"To have faith is to lose your mind and to win God."*

In any case, our transition into being is quite disturbing as well, due to its arbitrary character, completely out of our control. We are simply born to the world without ever being aware of it and consequently having no recollection of it. This missed encounter with life, which is our birth, escapes us because it has been desired by *others.* In other words, it is the fallout of an animal instinct, a hormonal impulse out of a concern for the survival of the species. Yet we are told that we are the winners of the *"lottery of existence"* the chances of winning which are one in 400 trillion.

By the way, the same absurdity is valid for the other extremity of our existence, namely death, whereby when it happens, we are not there to meet it.

This means that we have no control over the essential stages of our existence, namely birth and death, and as a result we only endure the unfair and arbitrary nature of life. A frightening prospect that makes daily life unbearable. Hence, we tend to invent a more bearable version of existence according to which life would have a purpose and that we are not here just by coincidence. After all, unlike truth, fiction must make sense.

The Cognitive Cacophony

After a while we begin to become aware of our existence, i.e., to perceive and identify ourselves as an individual and in relation to others and the world. This also makes us aware of our dependence on others. And this is where all of our troubles begin, namely the sensation of being inhabited by *consciousness*, most probably an emergent property of the complex organization of matter in our brains.

Yet, despite its major relevance and consequent importance in shaping individual lives and the moral and political world, consciousness has no biological function. This has led some to regard it as the biologically useless by-product of certain brain processes. In other words, a kind of mental pollution produced by the activation of complex neural networks which is the main source of our existential problems. After all, without consciousness there would be no existential questioning.

While *being* is a subjective experience, consciousness drives us into existential questioning, starting by wondering whether there is a universal consciousness or is it only specific to us humans. A rather relevant question insofar, if matter is fundamentally unconscious, it would mean that we live in an unconscious and purposeless Universe. That would make us the only conscious beings in an unconscious, inanimate, and mechanical Universe.

It also generates a terrible feeling of alienation from the rest of the natural world. Moreover, believing the materialist account of consciousness, our minds are locked in our brains and our only connection to others is physical contact, resulting in a tremendous sense of isolation and separation.

Thus, while being our singularity compared to the other animals of the planet, our developed consciousness has become the essence of our existence. Moreover, it is a faculty that gives us the possibility of knowing our actions and the ability to evaluate and judge them. Yet, it is considered by many as the *"poisonous gift of the existence"* since it makes us become aware of our *Sisyphean condemnation*. The proof?

It is very simple, let us look at the animal world. They don't seem to be subjected to the same existential dilemmas, phobias, and neuroses as Man. Their life is quite simple, and run by their instincts, i.e., innate behaviors such as survival and reproduction. They do not need to control or inhibit their hormonal or physiological impulses. A simple and wild world without politeness and etiquette. However, we laugh at them and consider them unconscious machines, deprived of soul, and stuck in the present.

According to this reasoning, in the absence of the soul, an essence totally different from the body, animals would be governed only by their animal instincts, namely a kind of mechanical principle. In other words, instinct does not need to be conscious in order to function.

What distinguishes us from other animals is the fact that we own the most sophisticated form of consciousness. Moreover, it is precisely this astonishing complexity of human consciousness that makes things even more complicated. It turns out that we are actually not that conscious either. In other words, we are mostly controlled by our unconscious which apparently occupies an independent region of the brain and has its own mode of operation. By reacting autonomously, it is a kind of almost unlimited hard disk that stores intuitions, fears, phobias, and traumas that are innate automatisms. Thus, we are merely unconscious beings driven by our impulses!

This supposed omnipotence of the unconscious does not please at all those who believe in the notion of *free will*. According to them, if we are determined to act by unconscious causes, how can we call ourselves free. Moreover, if one is not free, how can one behave morally, since such conduct implies being able to choose between good and evil?

By free will, we obviously mean the notion of voluntary action, which is opposed to that of reflex. Are we truly at the origin of our actions, our choices, and our thoughts?

The importance of this question arises from the fact that it is difficult to envisage a human society without individual responsibility. If free will were disproved, it would have huge consequences for society, since all our laws are based on the notion of individual responsibility. In other words, by removing our responsibility, we would be free to fulfill the social contract or not. It would also mean that we could not be punished for any misbehavior, in the absence of free will, namely intention and action.

A frightening prospect, where everyone would cheat by taking refuge in the argument that we are not masters of our actions. As a matter of fact, we are neither absolutely free nor totally determined, but rather in a system of constraints, which leaves us a little room for maneuver.

We shape our lives by the choices and events we face throughout our lives. However, we are not in control of these life events, which are often beyond our control, because of their random character. This is where things get complicated. While we have the impression that we play a role in our *"destiny"* and influence it, the reality is something else. In other words, the choices we make follow a logic of their own. Thus, unconsciously, our choices are influenced by our physical and our psyche, which are hereditary elements and thus out of our control. In other words, from a sociobiological point of view, the genetic baggage of the individual and the so-called genetic determinism would be behind all human behavior and not his free will. It seems as if we are condemned to suffer a destiny that does not leave us much room for maneuver.

To sum up, one thing is sure, free will is only possible if we are able to dominate our unconscious. However, considering the fact that our physical and psyche are out of our control, the only choice left is to try to understand our reactions to external impulses and by acting differently, to make the best of each given situation. Is that free will?

The Sexual Farce

We live despite all the hassle and without really knowing why. There seems to be a mysterious force hidden within us that drives us to stay alive and perpetuate life. Sexuality is one of its pillars leading to an animal and irrational desire to mate and to perpetuate the human race and serve life.

As is the case with all human dimensions, our sexuality, unlike other animals, has evolved into a complex and multidimensional phenomenon. While animal sexuality is only determined by genetic and biological mechanisms, human sexuality has emotional, relational, and cognitive dimensions. In other words, it includes biological sex, sexual identity, sexual orientation, eroticism, pleasure, intimacy, psychological well-being, and reproduction.

This animal instinct has turned into a major aspect of our identity, providing us with intimacy, love, tenderness, and affection. In any case, we have not much choice and programmed in our operating system, a hormonal impulse pushes us towards the opposite sex and leads to coitus.

Yet, we have managed progressively to dissociate sexuality from hormonal cycles, which has led to the appearance of non-reproductive sexual activity. Consequently, the goal of human sexuality is no longer copulation, but pleasure.

As for the cognitive dimension of human sexuality, we have complicated things horribly and by adding rational and ethical aspects to the equation. This deviation from nature, i.e., the determinism of reproduction, has made us responsible for our sexuality.

Nature's ruse to force us to engage in sexual act is based on the notion of pleasure. We are trapped in a perpetual loop of *desire-pleasure-enjoyment*, which puts us in a permanent race to satisfy desire through pleasure. Our fuel in this quest is *dopamine*, the influx of which induces a state of activation of the body and mind. Thus, desire is neither rational nor ephemeral, and satisfiable.

Desire is the engine that keeps us going. However, the tragedy of human desire is its selfish nature which at first obsesses us, but then seems absurd the second it is satisfied. In other words, human desire cannot be fulfilled and once one has acquired the desired object, one stops desiring it and the desire moves on to new objects. Apparently, this paradox is due to the fact that we do not desire a thing because it is good, but what makes it good is our desire to possess it. Thus, being by nature irrational and obsessive, its psychic hold on us alienates and enslaves us.

Apparently during our millennial fermentation, our sexuality has turned into an aberration, leading to behavioral disorders and mental diseases These disorders include exhibitionism, fetishism, frotteurism, pedophilia, sexual masochism, sexual sadism, voyeurism, etc. As for the origins of these sexual deviances, according to psychoanalysts we are all, more or less sadomasochists, because of their presence in infantile sexuality. It's quite striking to see how blurred the border between pleasure and madness could be.

The sexual madness of mankind has no limits and we have even turned it into merchandise. By transforming a natural instinct into a lucrative industry, we have truly surpassed all other animal species on his planet. Yet this has also other drawbacks such as porn addiction that can lead to physical, mental, psychological, and social problems. These include behavioral disorders such as obsessive-compulsive behavior, anxiety, sexual dissatisfaction, and even nervous breakdowns.

The Moral Farce

While our natural temperament leads us to freedom, we superimpose on our original nature a second one called morality, even though it limits our freedom. These set of rules of conduct and values, such as politeness or civic mindedness, aim at repressing our natural impulses, which could endanger the survival of the group.

Morality also helps us in our quest to distinguish ourselves from the rest of animal kingdom. In any case, the foundations of human morality are to be found in the innate capacity of the genes to favor behaviors that ensure the preservation of the greatest possible number of genes in the species. Some philosophers join this interpretation of classical morality by calling it our *"herd instinct"*, i.e., our inability to emancipate ourselves from the masses.

We submit to moral values because of our inability to live alone (*weakness*) and in order to avoid chaos and preserve the survival of the species through social peace. These rules of conduct regarding good and evil are imposed both on the individual and collective conscience. They include tolerance, respect, loyalty, and discipline. Being the rules of value, they are based on a division of acts into good and evil. In other words, good is what is desirable and value-generating, a kind of karma that contributes to happiness. Evil, on the other hand, is everything that is undesirable, such as pain, illness, and death.

Some radical philosophers, like Nietzsche, have challenged the objectivity and transcendence of human morality. They reject the traditional and religious criteria of good and evil because they lock us into a soothing ignorance. According to this school of thought, religious morality promotes suffering by devaluing life on Earth. Instead, they propose a complete reversal of moral values, and a kind of liberating nihilism that aims at transfiguring us into supermen, who are the beings that despise reactive morality, happiness, virtue, and compassion and who blossom in freedom of mind and creation. So, the recipe for becoming superman is to reject dualistic metaphysics, namely the separation between our world and that of the Gods and souls. Moreover, it assumes to want to know reality as it is, with its share of chance, evil, unpredictability and absurdity.

Once again, we end up in an existential aporia with regard to the origins of good and evil. Are we intrinsically good or evil? If we were naturally good, why would we need moral education? Socio-biologically speaking, while the aggressive behavior, dominance, and group territoriality of the animal kingdom, would have been imprinted in the brain of humans, the millenary evolution of mankind seems to have succeeded in mitigating the manifestations of these genes and in favoring the behaviors that ensure the preservation of the greatest number of genes in the group.

In other words, by dint of having been obliged to live in groups, we have developed empathy and the ability to put ourselves in the place of our fellow men and to treat them as a fellow human being. Yet we see the opposite namely the natural wickedness or cruelty of Man, manifesting themselves in monstrosities, such as torture, incest, rape, pedophilia, murder, etc.

Obviously in our daily lives we do not see the supposed original capacity for goodness in mankind and it seems to have disappeared. One would even be tempted to assume that violence and aggression are integral and innate part of humans. To some philosophers all acts of violence would be committed out of ignorance (error of judgment) and therefore involuntarily. As for the remedy, they advocate education and culture as a bulwark against barbarism. According to this hypothesis, violence should be limited to the less civilized parts of the Earth. However, the bloodiest wars of the 20th century were initiated in the more cultivated part of Europe and the campaigns to raise the awareness of young people since then have not really changed much. The breakthrough of the far right and other extremist movements in Europe is proof of this. Moreover, after decades of awareness campaigns, we only see a trivialization of violence and the rise of extreme parties on the political spectrum. Perhaps, after all, we have to recognize the fact that we are impulsive beings and violence is deeply human and cannot be eradicated. While psychoanalysts consider violence to be an unconscious human impulse (drive), sociobiologists believe that it has its roots in the more distant past where half of the mammals often resort to violence to resolve conflicts. In other words, we have a genetic predisposition to kill each other!

Today's civilized human societies do not seem to have escaped this genetic inheritance either, and one could ask whether wars, genocides, xenophobia and ethnocentrism are a transformation of the protective instinct of individuals towards their tribe?

If we believe the philosophers of evil, Man would be the battlefield where the struggle between good and evil takes place. It is therefore not a question of eliminating evil but of trying to maintain it in balance with good. The acceptance of this multiplicity which composes us, will bring us to lucidity and peace of heart. After all, Man needs the worst in him if he is to achieve the best. Hence the famous quote from Jung: *"No tree can grow to heaven unless its roots reach down to hell."* Consequently, the assumption that Man is naturally good does not make sense. It is better to stop wanting the good without the bad and the light without the darkness. We are responsible for our actions since they influence global reality.

Our millennial civilization presupposes and implies among other things a certain level of cultural and moral maturity. This requires a greater personal and collective responsibility in our choices and by putting aside shortcuts and the binary vision of things. We should stop imposing ideas to reality and adopt a more consequentialist approach to moral norms. Why not favor an epicurean pragmatism by giving more importance to the "context" in evaluating the usefulness of any moral rule?

By making all the necessary and nuanced distinctions, this new approach will allow us to think more directly in terms of what makes an act moral. Put differently, a more critical and practical interpretation of rules, where the barometer would be to see how much an act improves life or reduces suffering.

As for morality in a world in full effervescence in all respects, it sends us contradictory signals. On the one hand, the world today is much more moral in the sense that wars and murders are less frequent, but on the other hand, we still have a long way to go towards racial, social, and economic equality. We only must look at the state of human relations, the increasing criminality, the corruption in political circles as well as in the business world.

Our moral challenge in the 21st century is to balance our need for freedom with the need for certain social constraints to avoid chaos in an increasingly interdependent society. In such a scenario, human rights will go hand in hand with human responsibilities, to build a sustainable world. The future of morality will flourish in a world that allows free thinking, multiculturalism, and a healthy dose of skepticism to keep our existing beliefs in check.

The Romantic Farce

In a desperate attempt to deny our genetic proximity with other animals, we continue to invent new abstract concepts allowing us to glorify our species. Romance and love are among those human inventions aimed at disguising our sexual drive in a culturally acceptable form, or if you will, *the sublimation of carnal attraction between two mammals.*

This explains the fact that love is one of the greatest enigmas of the human condition. It makes us happy and dazzled, but at the same time miserable, confused, and vulnerable. Yet we continue to worship love the burden of which can easily ravage and destroy us.

This romantic obsession of us can even take on pathological proportions where the victim would get outright addicted to the feeling of love and need romantic partners to exist. Most probably, it is simply a dopaminergic and ephemeral chemical cocktail that often transports us to the heavens only to send us down into a hell of disillusionment and suffering.

This is confirmed by science which considers love a hormonal and pure biochemical phenomenon. Put differently, we are programmed genetically to love in order ensure the survival of our species. This is done by triggering a multitude of chemical explosions in the brain, making us attracted to the romantic partner. More precisely, by seeing the object of love, nervous messages are sent to the limbic system leading to a great chemical cocktail bringing an intense pleasure.

As it was the case with sex, there are several romantic pathologies in our post-modern societies. Toxic love, takes many forms, such as: emotional dependence, narcissistic or obsessive love, acute depression after a break-up, the inability to leave a violent partner, obsession with an unattainable person, etc.

As for the love-sex cleavage, we continue to consider them two different things belonging to two different spheres. In other words, while love is the feeling of having found the person who fulfills our dreams, sexual desire is based on the ability to imagine one's pleasure and to project oneself into its realization.

In the same vein, the proponents of this distinction between love and sex claim that the neural difference between love and sexual desire has remarkable overlaps and distinct differences. Thus, some surprisingly similar brain networks would be activated by love and sexual desire.

And last but not least, according to these love-worshippers, the fact that we can have sex with someone without loving him/her, demonstrates the fact that love and sex are two different things.

Yet, science has an explanation for romantic attachment, namely *oxytocin*. Also known as the love or attachment hormone, oxytocin is secreted during orgasm which in addition to pleasure and relaxation, sex provides a sense of connection.

So, it is believed that sex can lead to love and attachment. And so goes on the romantic confusion of mankind torn between the nobility and the purity of love and the animality of sexuality.

Faced with the elusive complexity of love, we are increasingly resorting to machines and technology. The idea is to quantify love and thus finally come to understand its nature and composition.

Whether it will work remains to be seen. One thing is though sure, namely that passionate love is irrational in essence and by crushing reason it escapes all theorizations. It is neither lasting, nor exclusive, nor unconditional. A mystical experience that makes us vibrate in a transcendent exhilaration to then make us sink into melancholy.

The Solitary Blues

Torn between solitude and multitude, the human dilemma of loneliness consists of choosing between getting gnawn away by oneself or the crowd.

For a long time, it was taken for granted that Man was not made to live alone, and so, haunted by the specter of exclusion from a group, everything was done to avoid rejection and isolation, whatever the cost. However, the welfare state and soon, the universal basic income, continue to emancipate and make us less dependent on others.

Thus, with this important rise of individualism in post-industrial societies, tolerating the caprices of others has become a real existential burden.

Broadly speaking, two opposing instincts act throughout our lives, namely the need for companionship and the need to be independent, separate, and autonomous. As a result, we often find ourselves oscillating between *withdrawal* and *participation* and the *quietude* and *anxiety* that the latter provide. This dualism or dilemma of mankind, i.e., to reject and venerate multitude at the same time, has most probably its roots in a discrepancy between our Darwinian heritage and the new circumstances of modern society.

Anyhow, our cosmic loneliness, i.e., feeling alone in a hostile universe, haunts us like a shadow from birth to death. Yet, it seems to be central and inseparable from human existence and consequently, it should be lived as a condition of our existence. Faced with this existential *"solitary confinement"*, we tend to escape it by resorting to hedonism, materialism, altruism, sensationalism, psychologism, theism, and love.

On top of our objective cosmic solitude, we also often suffer from its subjective versions. subjective versions, namely exclusion and social isolation where the person in question is not engaged in any relationship with others. This is often accompanied by anxiety, agitation, marginalization leading to physical and mental health issues and increased mortality. Feeling rejected and excluded can lead to depression and even suicide. These harmful forms of loneliness, favored by our individualized societies, often manifest themselves as a feeling of abandonment or social isolation.

The innate paradox of solitude is the fact that while giving birth to the original in us, it also generates the opposite namely the perverse, the illicit, and the absurd.

It seems to be a cocktail of psychological, cognitive, and emotional factors that everyone is trying to understand, compensate for and even anticipate. Whatever our age or social class, we are prisoners of human solitude. The proof: we are born alone, and no one will die in our place. However, we don't like this sad fact and repress it by whatever means at our disposal. We hide ourselves cleverly behind superficial relationships that ultimately fail to fill our voids.

The worst part in all that is the solitude gives us the impression of not existing. Perhaps, because as a mirror of the soul, solitude forces us to face our own company. A frightening prospect for those of us who can't stand themselves, so they would try everything to avoid this introspection and existential reunion with themselves.

Yet, by dissolving in a crowd, this existential curse does not always disappear and leads to the experience of *"loneliness within the crowd"*. Added to this is the "emotional loneliness" resulting from the lack of deep and enriching relationships with others, as well as its underlying version, i.e., romantic loneliness, often experienced by people, who do not have a close connection with their romantic partner.

Culture can also cause loneliness, partly among immigrants because of the absence of their culture of origin, but also in general due to the individualization or even atomization of modern societies. These latter trends, namely the most extreme forms of individualism, would threaten the very notion of society, which is becoming more and more a union of shared differences. So, in a Shakespearian manner one would ask: *"Solitude or multitude, that is the question"*.

Utopic Illusions

Faced with absurdity of life, we tend to seek refuge in Hope, yet it often amplifies our sufferings and makes us more harm than good, as a shadow over the future and the illusory field of possibilities. In short, hope is an antidepressant delaying the awareness of our ineluctable fall.

However, we continue to worship hope as a remedy against despair and fear. It seems to help us sustain through trials of faith, human tragedies and difficulties that might otherwise seem overwhelming. By all accounts, hope seems to be a human invention to face the cold indifference of the Universe towards us. We often end up realizing that we are surrounded by relativism, subjectivity and uncertainty between balance and permanent imbalance. This leads us to doubt and despair, our worst nightmares, even worse than sadness. Therefore, instead of facing reality with courage and lucidity, we decide to take refuge in a less tragic version of reality: the cult of Hope. We think that dreaming would calm our sufferings (neuroses), but by taking refuge in the future and sowing illusion, we often end up reaping these same sufferings. As a result, many philosophers reject hope, either because of its irrational or because they consider it an expression of a mistaken relationship to the world that is unable to cope with the demands of human existence. Hence, it prevents the intellect from grasping the truth.

Broadly speaking, the mere desire for something to happen can lead us to overestimate the likelihood of it happening to us, making most hopes to some extent false and illusory. These false hopes prolong our torment, leading to inevitable frustration, disappointment, and resentment. Thus, *a bitter truth is to be preferred to a false hope.*
By preventing engagement with reality, false hopes entrench an attitude of passivity and subservience. If one believes this hypothesis, hope is a curse since it immobilizes Man.

At first glance, in a world where our needs and desires are so often faced with uncertainty, hope comforts us by resting on the expectation of a better situation than the existing one. Yet, by relying on ignorance about the future, and by projecting ourselves into a future that is more positive than the present, we often condemn ourselves to disappointment. In other words, despair comes from hope, namely a non-fulfilled expectation, whereas by not hoping and expecting we can protect ourselves against despair and disappointment.

The cult of hope is merely the *"coloring"* of a tragic life. At the same time, hope is painful, because the desired thing is not yet within reach and, moreover, may never be. Added to this is fear, also known as the price of hope, which makes up the hope-fear pair. In other words, there is an element of fear in every hope, the fear that it will not be realized, and perhaps also a grain of hope in every fear.

Normally, this attitude should completely exclude hope since it demands that our forces be turned towards the present and not towards the future. However, for many people, it would seem quite difficult to free themselves completely from the tyranny of hope. Even Albert Camus ended up opting for the *"strange hope"*, i.e., a hope oriented towards the possibilities inherent in the present and characterized by humanism and solidarity with all human beings.

On a collective level, our penchant for hope often leads to Utopia, an idyllic society which in some ways is the most successful of civilizations. There is no shortage of examples, starting with Plato's republic and going through communism, fascism, and liberalism, we do not stop this quest for the ideal society. In the same vein, even John Lennon fell for the spell of hope and composed the song "Imagine" encouraging us to imagine a world of peace, without materialism, without borders separating nations and without religion. Let's imagine for a second such a utopia, a peaceful and fraternal world without poverty and inequality, without borders, without hatred, without violence, and full of pleasure and well-being. A society without dilemma and without contradiction, where we have all become eco-citizens living in harmony with others and nature. In other words, *the land of chimeras*, which according to the philosopher Jean-Jacques Rousseau is the only one worthy of being inhabited.

The problem with this human tendency, i.e., the cult of utopias, is the fact that often utopias turn out to be *dystopias*. The communist utopia, which was supposed to liberate man from exploitation and create a just society, turned into a totalitarian nightmare, and economic liberalism and free trade created the current chaos we are all more or less living in. Perhaps Immanuel Kant was right when he said, "*Nothing truly just can be built with such forked wood as man is made of.*" In any case, the ephemeral nature of our utopias should not surprise us since the word *utopia* in Greek means "*no place,* namely non-existent or even irrational or impossible. In other words, we imagine perfection, without considering the possibility of transposing this ideal to reality. The "*Land of plenty*" is a good example, an earthly paradise where nature overflows with generosity for its inhabitants and guests and where an ideal governor reigns over a happy people.

What is the point of creating a perfect society on an abstract level, knowing that it would never be transposable to reality? Is it its lack of pragmatism that is at fault?

Obviously, we are utopian animals who constantly try to displace reality in order to lift the burden of reality, without really wanting the ideal. Put differently, it tears us off from the present and awakens in us a concern of the future.

As for the dystopia, it also has a virtue, insofar as it allows us to become aware of the consequences of our actions and thus to keep the hope of change. Often, when faced with a dystopia, we tend to replace it with a new utopia. Thus, the communist dystopia has been replaced by the utopia of socio-economic liberalism. But this last one also ended up turning into a dystopia. Why did this happen?

Generally speaking, most utopias are based on good intentions towards mankind, however, often by insisting on conformity to a social model we make it repressive. It is therefore imperative to add an important dose of *relativism* and *pragmatism* to the formula. In other words, an attitude according to which the conceived ideal is not considered sacred and an immutable perfection. Consequently, it needs to be perfected and finetuned constantly by not excluding any possibility of its evolution.

Obviously, the quest for utopias continues and among its recent versions we find *feminism* and *environmentalism*, which by the way would not be the last ones. It seems that we are the utopian beasts secreting utopian hopes that in turn help us to find solutions to get out of the trap of the previous utopias/dystopias. This is also the recommendation of Rousseau who advises us not to give up the *ideal*. For him, we should not be satisfied with reality and continue the search of the *absolute*, i.e., something that does not need to exist to *be*. In his own words: *"There is nothing more beautiful than the non-existent!"*

The Happiness Farce

Faced with unbearable lightness of existence, Man has invented a new way out of this impasse, a state of grace called *happiness*. Yet we are not really able to precisely define it. What is happiness?

Is it those rare but ephemeral moments of euphoria, or rather something absolute like a state of mind or a condition?

The formal definition of happiness characterizes it with a *pleasant sensation where the mind and body are in a form of integrity, a state of complete satisfaction characterized by its stability and durability.* This means that it is not enough to feel a brief contentment to be happy.

While the above definition considers happiness as a lasting state, for some scholars happiness is only felt in the form of small moments of contentment and is therefore ephemeral. According to them, happiness could not be a permanent state since it would lose its value. Imagine for a second the horror of a perpetual orgasm!

Anyway, in a permanent quest to be torn out of ourselves, our lives have become a never-ending quest for distraction. We try by all means to obtain pleasant sensations. However, these are only ephemeral feelings that change with each instance and force us into a constant race to acquire more pleasant feelings and chase away the unpleasant ones. What is the point of striving for something so ephemeral?

Isn't this permanent quest of Man to find absolute happiness the very source of his unhappiness?

For some, happiness is synonymous with *power, wealth,* or *health.* Some even confuse it with *pleasure,* which in reality is only the satisfaction of a lack and only one of the components of happiness.

For nihilists, life is an absolute tragedy since it makes us oscillate between suffering and boredom.

Thus, the search for happiness is only a distraction from the ultimate absurdity of existence. The anti-suffering recipe of the nihilists consists in making life cease, i.e., stop procreating.

So, what is the secret of happiness, knowing that what can make us happy is just as capable of making us miserable?

Even in the midst of a positive feeling we are afraid of losing it. Thus, the *impermanence* of our feelings is the main source of our sufferings, namely this absurd quest for absolute happiness. It is perhaps time to stop this futile search and to free us from the tyranny of "absolute" happiness. Perhaps we should stop looking for happiness elsewhere, but rather in the depths of our lucid minds.

Happiness comes from within and not from thrills such as the one felt by a stoned junkie. So, the remedy consists of stopping seeing life as a *permanent evaluation* by knowing that as conscious beings, we can only fulfill ourselves by *being present* in the world. This would mean paying exclusive attention to the *present moment,* the power of which can make all our intrusive thoughts disappear and silence the mental noise inside us.

To purge our minds, we need to create the conditions for total attention to the present. By freeing ourselves from this *mental bulimia* and the compulsive thoughts that come from it, we will be able to access happiness and inner peace. Having said that, this would take a lot of patience and perseverance to get the desired result.

According to some others, it is possible to be happy and to achieve genuine happiness, since the needs of the body are both limited and easily satisfied. It is enough to put aside unlimited desires, without vital necessity, such as luxury and wealth. Thus, according to the Persian philosopher Omar Khayyam, it does not take much to be happy. According to this Persian recipe *"true happiness is a rose, two loaves of bread, three friends, four songs and five bottles of wine."*

The *Epicurean* account of happiness goes in the same direction namely, to bring one's desires within the limits of the body and its simple needs, and thus to be able to enjoy one's being. Thus, instead of suffering the tragedy of life, we could try to understand and *love it as it is without expecting it to love us in return.* With a relaxed, clear, and fulfilled mind, let's aim for serenity by living in the *moment* without fantasizing about the *better,* which is the enemy of *good*!

The Phantasm of Immortality

Let's imagine that we managed to reach authentic happiness, that does not relieve us from the anxiety of being mortal. Let's face it, we do not really live but rather survive, and as soon as we have recovered from the trauma of the birth, we must face the threat of death. As the horizon of life, death is the only certainty in a world of uncertainty. This finitude of the human soul haunts us all from birth, where our journey towards death begins. So, to be born is a pledge to die.

Most probably, we are the only animal on this planet to fear death, because of an *evolutionary error* that has given us a highly developed memory and a capacity for anticipation that has allowed us to become aware of our mortality. In animals, on the other hand, this awareness of a danger of death is rather punctual and does not last. Thus, once the danger has passed, normal life resumes its course and death is forgotten.

Generally speaking, as a void or nothingness, death is quite difficult to conceptualize. This difficulty comes from the fact that consciousness is the meeting of a subject and an object. Thus, it is a real impossibility for human consciousness to grasp its own nothingness. In other words, in the absence of the subject there is no object. Nevertheless, nothingness scares us, and we try to escape it by immortalizing ourselves.

According to some, if there is nothing after death, then there is no point in living. Consequently, we have invented religion in order to claim eternal life. According to most religions, Man is the result of a divine and elaborate plan and that he would not exist just by chance. Thus, we reconcile ourselves with our mortality, since faith makes us eternal, transfiguring death into a journey to a better world.

Whatever the truth, one Platonic fact cannot be denied, namely that the sensible world is the world of *corruption* and permanent *degradation*.
Thus, every second we lose our vigor, and our bodies wear out over time. In fact, after our conception, follows a long path of physical

transformations, starting with a metamorphosis of the initial cell, followed by childhood, youth, old age, and death. It seems that apart from external factors such as accidents and diseases, human life expectancy is somehow bound and decided by its genetic code and most human cells and organs have a maximum lifespan that is genetically pre-programmed.

While all living organisms on Earth follow the law of nature, which is the cycle of life, we try all possible tricks in order to avoid or postpone death. However, this obligatory passage from one season to another, i.e., birth, youth, old age and finally death, seems to be a fatality. After all, greening, blooming and finally wilting is an integral part of the natural beauty of life on Earth.

Scientifically speaking, immortality is now a technical problem and not an inevitability. More precisely, it would be achieved by blocking the mechanisms of cellular degeneration, which in the medium term could lead to an almost eternal life. In the meantime, some people are *cryogenically* preserved, which consists of preserving the body in cold, hoping to be brought back to life in the distant future. This obsession of Man to fight against his annihilation has contributed to the creation of a lucrative and flourishing market where high-tech companies are positioning themselves to make profits.

In the same vein, the quest for immortality continues through the technological path where transhumanists envision the *Augmented Man*, which consists of an improvement of the physical and mental capacities of humans via an advanced use of nano- and biotechnologies.

The fervent critics of transhumanism fear a fracture in humanity leading to the emergence of *biological castes*.

In other words, the capacity of infotech and biotech to restructure our bodies and our minds, could lead to the emergence of a new category of Man, namely the *Superhumans*. In other words, a new form of modern *aristocracy* where the rich being able to buy improved bodies and brains would dominate the rest of humanity, which is becoming increasingly redundant. In the absence of any economic or political power, the latter could risk being eliminated by the Supermen!

Science fiction or a real possibility, one thing is sure, human stupidity knows no limits and we must expect anything as long as we are led by testosterone-fueled primates!

While aging means a general weakening of all the organs of the human body, according to some philosophers, *the soul does not age.* In other words, there is a gap between the body and the mind that would be manifested by the suppression of certain passions and their replacement by others. Apparently, this idea is not shared by everyone and most of us have a negative attitude towards aging, which is often manifested by a feeling of fatigue and weariness.

As a result, old age is seen by many as a tragedy, even a handicap. However, let us not forget that each season has its charm, and that old age also has its virtues. Among these more joyful aspects of old age, we find the financial ease that would allow old people to be more active in the field of culture and leisure. Another privilege of age is the fact that one has no more the need to appeal to others.

As for our obsession with immortality, it might seem comforting, by mitigating the absurdity of existence, but on closer inspection, it is not a happy prospect.

Considering the fact that eternal life resembles a long boring river, wouldn't perpetual sleep be preferable to the agonizing prospect of living forever?

Moreover, the Earth will not be able to support this increase in life expectancy which will inevitably exhaust its natural resources. And finally, let's think about the young generation that in such a nightmarish scenario would have difficulty finding its place.

Perhaps it is time to change our perspective and look at this other extremity of the cycle of life positively. By not forgetting death we end up valuing and cherishing life more and consequently living each moment more intensely. Thus, it is a matter of *deriving some happiness from death*, since the knowledge of a truth is happiness in itself, even though it might sound bitter. After all we are better off with true sadness than a false joy!

As for the encounter with death, which terrorizes many of us, one should not ignore the fact that as long as we are alive, there is no death, and once it has arrived, we will no longer be there to feel it, or even encounter it. In other words, our relationship to reality exists only through our senses, so death is nothing since it would be the deprivation of all sensation. Let's imagine it for a second, death is to dissolve into the universe and to plunge into an eternal nothingness, a state of total appeasement of suffering, liberation from anguish, and perfect calm.

Let us not fear death, since it is soft and delivers us from the thought of death. This contingent certainly is the driving force of evolution, the beginning of renewal and the mother of diversity. It is not a finitude but rather a *re-commencement*. So, let us not consider it as a divine punishment since we owe our life to death.

This synthetic account of human existence leaves us perplexed as to the point of all that hassle. We are thrown into existence unwittingly and as such also condemned to a deterministic death. We struggle to survive and reproduce ourselves so that this bizarre cycle of life goes on. Maybe Schopenhauer was right after all?

Paradigmatic Absurdity

Since the dawn of time, Man has been searching for the *absolute* and *transcendental principle,* which governs and conditions a priori all possible experience. However, the philosophical, scientific, and religious paradigms invented so far have not yet succeeded in that.

In a generalized theoretical blur, we are witnessing a chaotic succession of incompatible systems whereby each paradigm brings us a new limited truth, which both denies and assimilates the previous paradigms. Thus, the *false* of today was the *truth* of yesterday.

This explains the huge number of existential paradigms of mankind which draw their roots in the subjective experience of the existence, by each one of us. Consequently, the exhausting quest for the absolute truth continues, and there is no sign of the much-sought absolute paradigm explaining everything and putting an end to our existential questioning.

Broadly speaking, the main concern in this endeavour would be the objectivity of all these attempts to clarify the mystery of life, which for the most part is biased. Moreover, as limited beings in all senses of the term, we are not sufficiently equipped to access the absolute truth if any.

First, because of our limited cognitive capacities which give us an incomplete idea of reality, namely a limited access to four space-time dimensions. Secondly, the principle of causality, well anchored in our brains, according to which every phenomenon would have a cause without which it is impossible for an effect to occur.

As a result, we end up in an infinite chain of causes and effects and thus makes us fall into aporia.

Man's intellectual arsenal can be summarized in three main categories, namely *religion, philosophy,* and *science.* While each having their own method in enlightening mankind, they can be described as paradigms, namely a representation of the world, or a way of seeing things. Paradigms are often broken down in disciplinary matrices, theoretical models, or schools of thought. Each of these "models of the world" is based on a defined foundation, which makes it inevitably subject to the limitations and distortions produced by their contextually conditioned nature.

Paradigms are important because they define the way we perceive reality and how we behave in it. Thus, some of life's great choices involve which paradigm to accept or reject. Yet, the imperfection of our paradigms has made us live in constant doubt since we know that sooner or later the dominating paradigm will be challenged by a new one.

This relativity of paradigms and value systems, unless proven otherwise, dissolves the notion of absolute truth and with a little luck, would incite the fanatics and dogmatists who claim to have a monopoly on absolute truth, to modesty. Besides, most of the international conflicts have their roots in the stubbornness of those who believes to have found the absolute truth. As a result, we continue to impose our values and thoughts on others and even go to extremes in this endeavour.

The history of humanity bears witnesses to this clash of paradigms, where we have killed each other for centuries for racial, political, religious, and ethnic reasons.

The Scientific Cacophony

Unlike religion, science is based on verifiable facts and seeks the assent of all its practitioners. Yet, its intrinsic limitation, i.e., not being suited to existential questions (why) has diminished significantly is authority in this field. Moreover, in its own domains, namely explaining the nature of physical phenomenon, it has not been quite convincing yet. For example, before Einstein, physicists considered Newtonian physics as the dominant paradigm governing physics. However, it was supplemented by Einstein's theory of relativity, which in turn was challenged with the advent of quantum mechanics. Consequently, because of this relativity of paradigms, a mixture of the theory of relativity and quantum physics is needed to explain cosmic phenomena. In the same way, modern physics today relies on these three theories to explain natural phenomena. Each of these paradigms seems to be valid for a specific domain. In other words, quantum physics at the nuclear level, Newtonian physics for everyday life and the theory of relativity at the cosmic level. Thus, a unifying cosmic theory is overdue.

The Religious Cacophony

Being lost in the limbo of existence, the cult of the gods has always been at the centre of our preoccupations and continues to be so in different forms. However, rationally speaking, it is rather a meta-rational leap beyond the reasonable and in some way a profound and impertinent illusion in our modern world. So, why abandon rationality in favour of a metaphysical approach to the Universe?

Is it a cry for love, a simply a dogmatic sleep freeing us from exhausting existential questions?

While science is based on verifiable facts and seeks the assent of all its practitioners, religion is dogmatic insofar as its answer to us is a revealed truth, imposed and established once and for all without us being able to discuss, criticize or question it. For religion, God cannot be proven, he is experienced and therefore faith does not lend itself to verification, which has led to its multiplication with very contrasting opinions from one religion to another.

By dramatizing existence and cultivating guilt, and by putting the Earth in inferiority with respect to Heaven, religion turns us away from life itself. Yet, we continue to crave for spirituality more than ever. The omnipresence of religion, even in the twenty-first century with so many technological advances, testifies to this.

Through the invention of religion, we have managed to calm several of our needs simultaneously, namely our need for certainty in a world of uncertainty, the fear of death and the glorification of the human species as something apart.   As a human invention, religion has come a long way from its primitive versions where human beings were sacrificed so that the gods would grant us mercy. Moreover, from polytheism to monotheism, under the influence of science and philosophy, religion has been forced to revise its teachings and adapt to its era. It has also known how to adapt to each era and continues to do so by constantly metamorphosing itself.

Yet, absurdly enough, the cult of the gods has turned into major handicap for humanity and contributing largely to our division. We have been fighting and killing each other on the basis of an irrational and metaphysical approach to the Universe. This trend was intensified after the transition from polytheism to monotheism, which as a totalitarian drift forcing everyone to worship the same God. Maybe, we were better off in the more tolerant polytheistic world where Gods could coexist peacefully.

Faced with the shortcomings of religion as an ideology of modern man, many of our intellectuals have tried, in vain, to reinvent religion by moving it away from superstition and transforming it into something both scientific and consoling. In other words, a secular and rational version to make up for the failures of religion. Thus, we find ourselves in a hellish impasse, namely the absence of a viable alternative to religious faith. This dilemma leads us to believe that perhaps the human brain is programmed to *"believe"*. Perhaps Voltaire was right when he said, *"If God did not exist, he would have to be invented."* So, this apparently intrinsic need of faith in mankind turns the idea of a world without religion into an illusion.

Many of us, faced with a hostile and cold world need a tranquilizer (faith) allowing us to keep hope and not sink into fear. In addition, for many, religion fulfills other needs such as: bonding with a community, healing, a moral framework for "lost" individuals or a scheme of thought and mediation. In the same vein, alienated by globalization, many people are separated from their long-standing local identities, and religion has stepped in to bridge this gap by providing a basis for identity and commitment that transcends national boundaries and unites civilizations.

The Philosophical Cacophony

Philosophy is the most critical and comprehensive thought process developed by mankind. It is situated between science and religion and while having the same goals as religion, i.e., to address our existential concerns, it uses a different approach. While religion relies on conviction and authority, philosophy relies on reason, reflection, and critical and rational questioning on all dimensions of human life.

Perhaps this hybrid nature of philosophy explains its relative lack of success compared to religion. In other words, by insisting on logical reasoning in pursuit of wisdom, it has somehow complicated things for itself.

While initially philosophy was somehow entangled with theology, with the coming of the *enlightenment*, it separated itself from theology and got closer to the new science. As a result, today philosophy relies more on science. However, the problem of this approach is that in metaphysics, or the nature of reality philosophy bumps into some obstacles. In other words, by relying on science and by claiming that the reality is physical it would have no method of dealing with other dimension to reality, i.e., abstract notions such as spirit and soul.

Another area of disagreement between religion and philosophy is the notion of morality where each of them tries to take ownership of it. For example, religion, by evoking its moral and ethical teachings such as love of neighbour and charity, claim that morality has always been religious. Philosophers contest this postulate and declare that Man, thanks to his reason, can establish morality without the support of faith. The secularized and laicized societies would be the living proof of this, they declare.

The religious counterattack by pointing their fingers at the alleged crisis of values and the loss of bearings in secular societies, which according to them is due to a decrease in religious influence in these secularized societies. In other words, they suggest that the disappearance of religion would be the moral apocalypse of humanity. Put differently, the absence of God leads to nihilism and pure and simple immorality, claim the religious.

It is true that we behave more morally when we feel observed, but this cannot be the only guarantee, preventing us from committing crimes. Moreover, the argument that the fear of being punished by God would lead humans to a more moral behaviour does not make sense. If this was really the case, the world would be a peaceful paradise, since a large majority of humanity identifies with a religious group. But this is not the case at all, and we are drowning in chaos and immorality.

And finally, the moral act is supposed to be selfless and not motivated by fear or an expectation of reward. Those who do not consider religion to be the foundation of human morality castigate the notion of sin, invented by religion to replace evil and thus dominate our consciences. A kind of dogmatic automatism that prevents us from contemplating the consequences of our actions. Thus, by introducing the notion of repentance, religion does not fight evil (sin), but somehow makes it reversible.

For centuries philosophers have delved into subjects such as the quest for truth and goodness, wisdom, and the art of living according to the good. Their method consists in reasoning, reflecting, asking questions, and trying to answer them in a coherent and argued way.

However, in the same way as religious doctrines, there is a permanent succession of incompatible philosophical systems where each one both denies and assimilates the previous paradigms. Considering the absurdity of the existence, and the inexhaustible nature of existential questions, even though they do not seem to get us anywhere, philosophy continues to delve into endless reasonings without being able to provide us the absolute truth.

The Tribal Absurdity

Since prehistoric times, humans as social animals have lived in groups, at first quite small and a kind of closed order that was designed to protect its members, bound to the group by blood. This is where we invented the word *stranger* meaning all those outside this closed circle which was the tribe. Our xenophobic paranoia starts then, looking at others with suspicion and considering them as potential enemies. This is the beginning of all the evils of mankind, since from that moment on, in an attempt to monopolize the resources vital to its survival, it was necessary to increase the power of the tribe, leading to intrigues, conflicts and wars. The rest, we know, gradually the tribes grew and the process of consolidation of tribes led to the birth of the first tribal societies and, later, to the creation of empires that collapsed one after another. And finally, the modern states as we know them today. All this has not changed the intrigues and wars, disguised as a new science called geopolitics.

This fragmentation and division of the human species is manifested by a planet divided into almost 200 countries and mankind is paying its price in shape of wars, violence, racism, xenophobia, global inequality, refugees, etc.

As for the unifying element of modern national states, we find factors such as race, language, culture, and history. Yet we are not that homogeneous within a nation either and seem to hold a portfolio of several identities, switching from one to another according to our needs. Put differently, we are in some way *Russian dolls* since we belong to several physical or virtual groupings, starting with the nuclear family, followed by the relatives and then member of an urban or rural community followed by professional and political orientation and finally the nation.

At first glance, the term nation refers to a human community that shares certain common characteristics, such as language, culture, religion, or history. However, today's nation states do not quite fit this definition. This is the case of the extended states that are made up of different communities.

These states have succeeded in imposing the same laws, regulations, language, and culture on a set of different populations. The latter claim to belong to a nation even though they depend on a geographically larger state. The Scots, the Catalans and the Basques are some examples of these where their nationalism is aimed at defending a culture oppressed or denied by an occupier or dissolved within a larger whole.

Another example of the ambiguity of the term nation in today's modern societies is the possibility of changing one's nationality through naturalization. It is even possible, in some cases, to have two or more nationalities.

The Nationalist Disease

Nationalism is a fairly recent phenomenon in the history of mankind which dates to the 16th century. At the beginning it was a liberation movement against dynastic and imperial dominations. It proclaimed the fundamental equality between citizens gathered within the same nation. This revolutionary and even romantic version of nationalism also appeared in the decolonization movements in Africa and Asia in the 20th century.

While nationalism was initially based on the historical, cultural, and linguistic unity of a population, it gradually metamorphosed into an aggressive expansionism leading to imperialism and colonialism. Thus, by considering the traditional values of a nation as superior to others, we witness a will to power, greatness, and domination, which translates into colonial expansion to open new markets or to access raw materials. Since then, nationalism has spread throughout the world, somewhat like a kind of secular religion in which the nation serves as a focus for the transmutation of religious symbolism.

In the same vein, a distinction should be made between nationalism and *patriotism* where the latter being a feeling of love and pride for one's country. Consequently, the patriot is ready to fight for it and to defend its interests. The excessive and aggressive version of patriotism is called *chauvinism* which systematically denigrates everything foreign. This unhealthy version of patriotism is expressed by an unconditional and exclusive admiration for what is national. Perhaps, after all, the French novelist Roman Gary was right when he said: *"Patriotism is love of one's own. Nationalism is hatred of others."*

As for the evolution of nationalism, it is to be noted that the wave of globalization that has swept the world since the last decades of the twentieth century has completely changed the situation. Political, economic, and social globalization marks the demise of national states and the beginning of a new era, characterized by the emergence of larger economic and political blocs such as the European Union. However, we observe that in the face of unbridled globalization, many people, alienated and marginalized, are demanding a return to the founding values of the nation. Thus, thanks to globalization and the resulting socio-political upheavals, nationalism is once again on the rise. Unfortunately, this often translates into withdrawal, xenophobia, and racism, as well as a desire for economic and cultural isolation.

The Culturist Dogma

The superiority complex does not limit itself to individuals and it has actually taken cultural proportions. In other words, today some cultures unashamedly consider themselves superior to the other ones.

Knowing that each culture, to a certain extent, has a subjective value, are there objective criteria to determine the superiority or inferiority of a culture? According to the *culturists*, yes. Unlike racism, which is rooted in biology and the supposed supremacy of the white race over other races, culturisme favors cultural values as superiority criteria. Based on this theory, the socio-economic and technological advances of the West can be explained by its culture that values reason, science and logic over faith or mysticism. Thus, cultures that value religion and associated beliefs often lag behind Western countries. Consequently, the Western civilization in a culturist approach promotes economic and political liberalism. However, the critics of the culturist theory contest these statements and declare that economic liberalism is in fact a devaluation of culture since it is done at the expense of the environment and people are not happier or more prosperous for that. For them, new technologies are only *money pumps* and killing machines and they therefore claim that a less developed nation with higher moral standards is superior.

As for democracy, its proponents claim that it empowers people and helps them to free themselves from the tyranny of the religious and the dictators. Yet, according to its critics, modern democracy is still a kind of repression that instead of constraining public opinion, manipulates it through the media. In other words, it is *a mature and successful dictatorship that uses soft power*, that is, *trying to influence rather than impose.* Maybe after all the Russian controversial politician Vladimir Zhirinovsky was right when he said: *"Dictatorship is constipation. Democracy is diarrhea. Choose what you like best."*

Democracy is thus a new *permissive system of domination* based on individuality, freedom, desire, and consent. It encourages us to obey our impulses instead of prohibiting them. Funnily enough, the desire which used to be a taboo has become a totem, namely an object of worship. So, who is right?

To answer this question, we need some objective criteria to be able to compare cultures. While technically, all cultures are relative, there are certain criteria that some cultures favor leading to the well-being and prosperity of their citizens. For example, it would not be wrong to consider women's rights, freedom of expression and economic development as criteria for evaluating a culture. Other criteria include the importance of the individual in relation to the group (society) and the right of everyone to life, liberty, property, and the pursuit of happiness. Ultimately, cultures differ in their sense of the greater good, that is, in their value system.

In contrast to nature, culture is a human invention. It is an umbrella term that encompasses the behavior and social norms of human societies, including their achievements such as their knowledge, practices, art, etc. Basically, culture is the manifestation of how we think, behave and act. In the same vein we find the term *cognitive style* which refers to the dominant way in which people in a culture conceptualize information. This produces a specific cognitive and cultural orientation that in turn results in observable behaviors. So theoretically, if we understand the cognitive style of another culture, we can understand why they may behave differently than we do and predict their reaction to our behaviors.

The next relevant term in this context would be the notion of *civilization*, which refers to the organized development of one or more cultures in an urban center. In other words, while culture embodies our thoughts and customs, civilization is a kind of urban settlement and is therefore not nomadic. A culture becomes a civilization if it has the following elements: language, science, technology, and a complex political system. For this reason, not all cultures have developed into civilizations. Therefore, a culture can develop and exist without civilization. As for the difference between civilizations, they differ from each other, by their main constituents which are history, language, culture, tradition and, above all, religion. It is precisely the enduring nature of the latter that explains the longevity of civilizations.

Having said that, every civilization seems to have a life span and they decline and disappear after a certain time. The causes of the collapse of civilizations are multiple, such as structural, socio-politic, and financial, but also natural disasters, famine, wars etc. The longevity of some is a result of optimal management of their territories, but often they become too large and in the absence of modern means of communication, control of their territories becomes impossible. This is the beginning of their decline, a period during which the balance of power changes and ends with the fall of the dominant civilization in favor of a newcomer.

By applying this theory of the decline of civilizations, we can better understand this supposed morphology of civilizations and their life cycles. Thus, the Arab-Muslim civilization would have reached its apogee in the Middle Ages, dominating intellectually, technically, and scientifically the West, which at the time was held hostage by the Christian religion. The advent of the Renaissance changed the situation and since then the Muslim world has given way to the Western civilization, boosted by the philosophers of light and the industrial revolution. The latter, thanks to its political-economic system and market capitalism, dominated the world until the end of the 20th century. However, its decline is beginning to be felt in the face of increased globalization and the emergence of transhumanism.

Is this a fatality or can Western civilization be saved? According to the optimists, it is quite possible to reinvent the West, while the more pessimists consider the decline of Western civilization inevitable. Applying the triplet of the dialectic plan, one would be tempted to consider Western civilization as the *synthesis* of Greco-

Roman civilization (*thesis*) and Judeo-Christian civilization (*antithesis*), whose decline had already begun with the Renaissance.

Faced with this decline of the West, intellectuals try to explain it by various theories and hypotheses. The American political scientist Samuel Huntington approaches this subject from the angle of a *Clash of Civilizations*. According to him, while the last two centuries were marked by imperialist and ideological wars, this century is supposed to be dominated by a culture war or even a clash of civilizations. In other words, cultural and religious identity would be the main source of conflict in the post-Cold War era. If this is true, and that the main axis of conflict in the future will be cultural, then we should be concerned since cultural characteristics and differences are less mutable and therefore less easily compromised and resolved than political and economic ones.

The critics of the above-mentioned hypothesis (Francis Fukuyama & Co.) evoke *the end of history*, a hypothesis according to which human rights, liberal democracy and the capitalist market economy have become the only ideological alternatives left for nations in our post-Cold War world. In the same vein, there is already talk of a universal civilization as a spin-off of increased institutional globalization. After all, nowadays we share almost the same conception of politics, economics, and science.

The question is whether this globalization would lead to a diffusion of norms, social practices, and values? Will it lead to acculturation and the cultural and civilizational unification of the world? Are we going to live in a single global civilization, like a melting pot that would transform everyone into a common mold?

The defenders of this *melting-pot view* put forward the idea that the development of information technologies, the increase of international exchanges and the rise of tourism and immigration would be the source of this global civilization. If this is true, we should expect a worldwide sharing of values, practices, beliefs, and even orientations. But is this really the case?

Proponents of global civilization mention Pizza and Burger that have become the world's staple food as a symbol of universal civilization. Another example of this global unification through sports would be sporting events like the Olympics and the World Cup of soccer. So, what can we expect? The clash of civilizations or rather the fusion of civilizations?

By looking at the post-Cold War international conflicts and their nature, one notices the emergence of new regional superpowers trying to assert themselves and get their share of the power in the new world order to come. Even more so, these global conflicts are increasingly manifesting themselves at the level of civilizational divisions. Clearly, globalization has not led at all to the leveling of cultures, but on the contrary to a world that is more than ever multi-polar and multi-civilizational. Why is that so?

The critics of global civilization claim that migration and the development of exchanges is not synonymous with a universal civilization, but that they would, on the contrary, increase the attention that one pays to one's civilizational identity. More precisely, as economic regionalism develops, it will increase *civilizational awareness*, which means the awareness of the differences between civilizations and the commonalities within civilizations.

As for the harmonization of our eating and sporting habits, according to the opponents of global civilization, this would be more the result of *Westernization* than of globalization in general. Moreover, this supposed cultural domination of Western civilization has had its limits and has not entirely influenced the fundamental cultural values of these Westernized societies. Japan is a good example of this; where after a certain period of fascination with Western culture, it has been able to recover and preserve its specificities.

Broadly speaking, our approach to cultural identity is more of a balancing act in which we try to find a balance between identification and differentiation, both within a group and between social groups themselves. Applying the same principle on a global scale, we find that the interaction between cultures is more *integrative* in nature than *assimilation* and dissolution into a global culture.

To better understand the mechanism of cultural integrations, we must begin with the real nature of culture. Culture is part of group survival mechanisms. It embodies the social codes designed to guide the behavior of individuals and thus their interpretation of the world. Thus, it functions as a filter where our cultural code defines our reality and determines our judgments. This explains the subjectivity of culture and its variations around the world.

The uniqueness of each culture lies in the fact that it has distinct patterns of thought, emotion, and behavior to survive in a given environment. That said, it is at the same time flexible, which allows us to adapt and survive in almost any socio-ecological environment on the planet.

Coming back to the alleged clash of cultures, it should be noted that it manifests itself on two levels: firstly, on the geopolitical scene followed by cultural conflicts within the same country due to increasing immigration to the West.

As for the geopolitical dimension of the clash of civilizations, while during the Cold War the world was bipolar, today the situation has completely changed, and the geopolitical landscape has become multipolar. Although the latter is dominated by the Sino-American antagonism, we must not forget the other major players in the geopolitical game, such as Russia, the Muslim world, etc. In the same vein, we must question the nature of these antagonisms. More precisely, is the Sino-American rivalry a cultural difference between Confucianism and Western liberalism or rather a power struggle to gain cultural and economic hegemony in the world?

For some, the main conflict between the civilizations is more ideological and takes the form of a confrontation between Western Christian civilization and the Muslim world. The problem with this hypothesis is the fact that the Arab-Muslim civilization does not provide any answers to the current challenges of humanity. In fact, the rise of political Islam in some parts of the world is not because of its superiority but rather due to the weakness of Western Judeo-Christian civilization in the face of the socio-economic upheavals of the world.

The other aspect of the clash of cultures, which is the one within the Western countries, is perhaps the more virulent and visible one. Migration flows from South to North have aggravated this cultural antagonism between immigrants and their host countries. This brings us to the subject of cultural assimilation. Historically speaking, the encounter of cultures often produces one of the following patterns. It either leads to the domination of one over the others; or turns into an integrative encounter based on complementarity and putting all participating cultures on an equal footing; and finally, the crossing or hybridization of cultures leading to the appearance of a new mixed culture. The latter implies the mixing of several distinct cultures leading to the production of a third and new culture with new standards. Brazilian culture is a good example of this, where there is a strong mixture of Portuguese, African and Amazonian Indian traditions.

The immigration to the West was initially intended for reasons such as the shortage of labor for industrial development or for reconstruction after the two world wars. In addition, there was also a need for making up for the demographic deficit and finally some waves of immigration by refugees from Eastern Europe and Russia.

Today's immigration towards the West is unwanted and triggered by political, socio-economic, or climatic crises. In most cases, it is immigration from underdeveloped countries to the developed part of the world.

Once in the host country, there are two main models of integration: an *assimilationist* model and an *integrationist* or *multiculturalist* one. The assimilationist model refers to the total abandonment of the immigrant's culture of origin, whereas in the integrationist model, widespread in Anglo-Saxon countries, the immigrant is invited to preserve and maintain his or her culture of origin, without this endangering the cultural and linguistic monopoly of the culture of the host nation. Thus, the religion, culture and language of minorities can be expressed freely in their private sphere, but the manifestation of these particularities in the public sphere will be suspected of undermining the social cohesion and values of the majority. As for these *values of the majority*, let us not forget the fact that they are also the result of a long (forced) process of homogenization, i.e., political, cultural, and linguistic unification, which has been accompanied by the suppression of regional languages, the division of territories to break the attachment to the old provinces, etc. This would explain the implicit or explicit expectations of host countries with regard to immigrants who are called upon to integrate into the culture of the majority.

Another point of divergence between the two main models of integration is the role they attribute to secularism. Specifically, for multiculturalism, inspired by American law, secularity serves to protect religions from the state, whereas in France, for example, it must prevent any religious interference in the functioning of the state.

Anyway, for some time now and in the face of poorly controlled immigration, the rise of terrorism and Islamic fundamentalism, multi-culturalist models have been increasingly criticized and associated with communitarianism. These critics propose a more assimilationist approach, however, the latter faces several obstacles due to its non-politically correct nature and its non-compliance with international human rights laws.

Clearly, the two dominant models of immigrant integration no longer correspond to the reality of the 21st century. What if we started thinking outside the box and adopted a hybrid approach?

In other words, we should invent a new system of integration by combining the best of both models. A new system of integration which is assimilationist towards immigrants within the framework of a society that favors the preservation of the particularities of each.

Thus, based on values such as freedom and tolerance, we could perhaps resolve the world's cultural conflicts and unite humanity. This could be achieved by freeing ourselves from *political correctness* and addressing the most difficult issues in a serene manner, while refraining from prejudging immigrants on the basis of their culture of origin.

As usual, it is a balancing act by which one must aim for the right balance, namely neither cultural relativism nor ethnocentrism, which is the belief in the superiority of one's own culture. It is thus a *measured cultural relativism* which would consider the cultural context in the evaluation of a different culture. This would make them seem less bizarre, offensive, or deficient to us. That said, we should not endorse the moral legitimacy of any cultural practice.

It is not a matter of reluctant tolerance but rather of cross-cultural criticism and firm rejection of any deviation from fundamental values such as human rights violations and terrorism. In these hard times, humanity needs more than ever the *cultural intelligence* that lies halfway between total acceptance and reluctant endurance.

The Identity Cacophony

Nowadays, we often hear the word identity and the fear of losing it. It is a notion with many meanings and dimensions, i.e., biological, cultural, and psychological. However, the essence of identity is what marks our uniqueness, that is, how an individual is different from others. To this is added the collective entity that distinguishes a group from others. In the context of a nation, national identity refers to a human community with a linguistic, historical, cultural, or religious identity.

Let us start with language, which is a major unifying factor within human societies. Language in itself is only a communication tool. Yet we tend to make it sacred and a vital survival mechanism. Yet, as human tribes continue to merge and create larger entities, the number of languages diminishes accordingly. This decrease is amplified by phenomena such as globalization, rural exodus, immigration, etc. This does not please some of us who fear the loss of a human heritage, as well as the loss of the knowledge captured by these languages.

This nostalgic or even romantic approach to language, making it a richness, is not entirely justified. The multitude and variety are not always enriching. One could rightly ask: wouldn't there be fewer divisions among humanity if everyone spoke the same language?

As for history and culture, we humans have this weird need to feel proud of our origins and identify with something beyond our own achievements, if you will, to anchor our identities behind our egos.

Broadly speaking, most of us have a substantial conception of identity, also called *innatism, which* claims that the mind is born with ideas, knowledge, and beliefs. As a result, the identity would be an abstract entity called *self*. Yet, this seems to be an illusion, considering the fact that we are nothing but a collection of perceptions. In other words, our identity is a pure construction independent of our innate attributes and the product of our interactions with the world. Consequently, identity is not innate but acquired. Sociologically speaking, our identities are just a collection of different perceptions, depending on the conditioning we have been subjected to.

However, as the mark of our uniqueness, identity should signify how an individual distinguishes and differentiates him or herself from others. The only thing that makes an individual unique is his or her genome, since no two individuals are completely alike on a biological or psychological level. The rest is tribal conditioning and, a factor of religious, political, cultural, ethnic, and sexual division.

Nowadays, identity is more about group conformity and contributes to the tribalization of the planet. This supposed richness, so venerated by our intellectuals, is the very reason for the rise of nationalism and the withdrawal.

In search of purpose and support in an increasingly uncertain world, people look for assurance in religion and the nation which in turn divides humanity.

The Global Village

Growing globalization since the 1980s, has accelerated the flow of goods, services and skills and has largely contributed to the reduction of poverty in the world, where more than two billion people have been pulled out of extreme poverty. Improved access to employment, nutrition, sanitation, and public health have contributed to an increase in the average life expectancy of the world's population.

However, during the same period, the capacity of international institutions to regulate globalization has been systematically undermined and they have failed to deal with the negative effects of globalization. This has led to growing mistrust among Western populations and the emergence of populism and nationalism calling for border closures and protectionism.

It goes without saying that the complexities of globalization will not be resolved by calls for nationalism and protectionism, however as long as there is such a huge gap of trust between rulers and citizens, one cannot expect anything better. This lack of trust in democracy, combined with economic problems constitutes a dangerous cocktail and it will have far-reaching implications for the political and social stability of the world.

As the world becomes more globalized and therefore more connected, it also becomes more fragile and interdependent. This is the flip side of globalization which, if not managed intelligently, will inevitably lead to more severe and increasingly more dangerous systemic risks.

A good example of this kind of systemic crisis is the financial crisis of 2008, where the negligence of governments and experts in dealing with the growing complexities of the global financial system, led almost to the collapse of the world economy.

We live in a global village which has made us interdependent and therefore more fragile. In other words, a reverse and negative "butterfly effect" revealed by the Covid-19 pandemic. This requires a coordinated and global response, namely an overhaul of all our major paradigms. In other words, we need to reassess our economic, social, and environmental systems and the way we think.

By thinking in silos, we often tend to forget about interdependencies. It is therefore necessary to approach our global challenges with more nuance and to consider them. holistically Looking at the history of mankind, we realize that we have never learned the lessons of the past.

World War II, in a way, was the direct result of mistakes committed by the post-World War I rulers, and oddly enough, we have continued the same path. The Cold War was also a consequence of World War II and now we seem to have revived it by humiliating and alienating Russia for the last thirty years. As this was not enough, we have added a new conflict to the menu, namely that of the Sino-American antagonism. We seem to be going in a vicious circle, repeating the same mistakes in a different form. In these difficult times for mankind, the last thing the world needs is division and rivalry. We need unity more than ever, so that we can act collectively to build a new world order that will ensure inclusive economic growth, prosperity, and security for all.

What matters most is human solidarity and empathy to build shared prosperity and a more inclusive, united, and sustainable world.

The Individual Nomadism

It should be noted that the wave of globalization that is sweeping our planet is going to lead to *the demise of state ideology* and hence mark *the end of national states* as we know them today. In other words, political, economic, and social globalization will herald the beginning of a new era, characterized by the emergence of larger economic and political blocs such as the European Union.

Some go even further and announce that after a period of chaos, the planet will become a unique entity, without borders, that is to say a kind of *transhuman* and *universal democracy* at the service of mankind. This is the hypothesis of the French thinker Jacques Attali who approaches the subject from the angle of *nomadism*.

According to hypothesis, nomadism has been the founding element of civilization and thus *sedentariness* is only a brief parenthesis in human history. It is true that for 5 million years, up to 8,000 years B.C., we were nomadic and on the move in pursuit of game or in search of fruit trees. The passage from nomadism to sedentarism took place with the birth of agriculture about 8000 years before Christ, which in its turn, favoring sedentarism, led to conflicts and wars for the defense of the territory.

According to this nomadic account of human societies, the technological advances of mankind have facilitated a new form of *individual nomadism*. The latter differs from its primitive version in that it would mean the disappearance of the notions of nomad and sedentary where each one would respect the other.

In the same vein, this transhuman narrative of mankind claims that *decline of sedentarism* has its roots in its innate *immobility* and *inward-looking attitudes*. Thus, it no longer corresponds to the challenges of humanity in the 21st century. Individual nomadism, on the other hand, thanks to its qualities such as its sense of innovation and freedom, is more adapted to the challenges of the planet and has all that is needed to guarantee stability and dynamism in the long term. According to this theory, the nomadization of mankind would mark the end of the *American empire* as *the last sedentary empire* in the world and with no room for any another one. Put differently, just as the Roman Empire succumbed to barbarian nomads, the American Empire will be undermined by the pressures of the three great nomadic forces, i.e., *market, religion,* and *democracy.*

The outcome of the *third globalization,* according to Jacques Attali, would be a trans-human democracy on a planetary scale, namely an amalgam between the virtues of the nomad and those of the sedentary. By the way, we already see it manifesting itself in different shapes such as work nomads, immigrants, refugees, expatriates, and migrants of all kinds. Thus, one billion individuals travel each year for pleasure or necessity, within their countries to exercise their profession or to look for it.

The new individual nomadism, based on individual freedom, will translate into *the right to change one's mind* and thus leave a place, a job, a country, or a family. This means a reversibility of all choices and the abandonment of constraints previously imposed by values such as justice, solidarity, faith, or dignity. We will thus witness the appearance of a new type of citizen, a nomad who obeys only his own whim and is constrained only by his own financial resources. More precisely, whereas in the first nomadism, the journeys were carried out in the service of the others, in the modern nomadism everyone becomes an obstacle even a competitor to the journey of the others. This would lead to the exacerbation of egoism, the obsession with personal success and the glorification of solitary pleasure, as well as the rejection of any collective responsibility.

The impact of such a change of mentality will be felt everywhere and thus the criteria for judging people, products and relationships will be more and more ephemeral and immediate. This will render the notion of commitment to something temporarily. Everyone is free to change suppliers, employers, partners, and religions at any time. Therefore, in order to maintain a private or commercial relationship, one must be able to offer one's partner something new. This *tyranny of the new* constantly calls into question the object of our investment. Consequently, it will inevitably also impact the economy whereby companies will become more and more precarious, mobile, and nomadic.

However, the dialectic of civilizations teaches us that this return of humanity to its founding nomadism could take more evolved forms and will not necessarily be limited to physical displacement. We can already see this, thanks to the technological advances that have made remote meetings possible. This obviously does not stop there and thanks to technologies such as augmented and virtual reality, we are going to reach virtual nomadism, i.e., remote hologram- and virtual journeys in 3D including smells and touch.

Such a metamorphosis of nomadism could lead to the emergence of new classes of nomads, namely a minority of luxury nomads with access to all the realities of the world, followed by a large group of virtual nomads, with virtual access to the delights of the world, and finally the nomads of misery, condemned to move constantly in order to find something to survive.

Another important aspect to consider is the environmental constraints such as the fight against global warming which will inevitably reduce physical movements and will lock us in *self-sufficient urban centers*. Would this be the end of classic tourism and the consumption of exotic products? We can also wonder about the long-term effects of such a slowdown of physical movements. Won't they lead to isolation and withdrawal, where people could barricade themselves in their territories and close themselves off from each other?

The critics of Jacque Attali's theory challenge the stigmatization of sedentary life which according to them was the very basis of civilization. While Attali considers the nomads at the origin of innovations such as the domestication of fire, clothing, hunting, tools, art, languages, music, painting, etc., his critics attribute them to sedentarism. For them, nomadism is synonymous with barbarism, savagery, and the enemy of civilization. Besides, the Roman Empire fell under the attacks of the barbarian nomads. For these critics, this chaotic vision of the world would lead to the division of humanity into three opposing groups, namely a ruling class composed of *hyper-nomads* followed by residual groups of sedentary people and a growing mass of *infranomads* condemned to forced mobility and precariousness. Thus, they see a future marked by violence and chaos. So, what shall we expect, a multi-civilizational world made up of sedentary empires or rather a unified and transhumanist world?

The Future of Nation

It goes without saying that, as social animals, we need the security of belonging to a group. After all, since ever, in order to flourish we need to be rooted in intimate communities without which we feel lonely and alienated. Political parties and the nation have tried in vain to fulfill this role without much success. This need for roots and community has been particularly amplified by the socio-political upheavals and globalization that have led to the disintegration and dislocation of human communities. Alienated and marginalized by global capitalism, we fear the loss of our national systems of social protection. This leads many of us to seek meaning and assurance in religion and in the nation. Populist movements aware of this need by relying on religion, culture, and national identity, take advantage of this situation to consolidate their hold on humanity. However, let us not forget that we have lived for millions of years without religion and nation. Instead of seeking reassurance from the latter, we would be better off to build a global community by strengthening the social fabric and bringing the world closer together. But how can this be done? Would technology do the trick?

Social networks will eventually be able to do it using AI. In other words, setting up tools capable of building communities by suggesting (via AI) the groups that make sense to their users. Given the global nature of our problems, global communities make more sense than the national tribe. The lack of depth of virtual communities should not discourage us from this initiative.

Anyway, in the face of the wave of chauvinistic ultranationalism that is sweeping the world, we have no choice but to use our imagination and common sense to unite our divided planet.

As for uncontrolled and illegal immigration, the current had-hoc measures are not efficient enough and doomed to fail. Immigration is a global problem and must be addressed as such. If current trends continue, global socio-economic inequalities, combined with the effects of global warming, will force us to resort to more radical measures. In other words, a two-pronged global migration policy.

Firstly, we must slow down the current population growth which if not stopped will result in more than eleven billion people in 2100. The Earth could not support such a global overpopulation. It is therefore necessary to accelerate the introduction of birth control measures in the poorest regions of the planet. At the same time, we need urgently to address the debt crisis of developing countries, which requires an international response. This crisis, which has been going on for forty years has been intensified by the financial crisis of 2008 and has completely paralyzed poor and indebted countries. The latter find themselves trapped in a vicious circle of blind fiscal consolidation, aimed at reducing their debt, which at the same time severely limits their ability to cope with future health and economic crises.

It is therefore imperative to react quickly and via an appropriate reform program, support developing countries and remedy the structural problems that have contributed to the vulnerability of the latter. Past experiences have shown that pro-market and austerity reforms will get nowhere. These measures have only intensified inequalities in the world and impoverished poor countries. The effective resolution of this financial plague would require a process of debt relief for these poor countries, focused on the objectives of sustainable development and on the sustainable economic growth of each country.

In parallel, we must also aim for *an organized redistribution* of the world's population from poor and overpopulated areas to sparsely populated areas such as Russia, Canada, Australia etc. Of course, this controlled immigration must take into account the characteristics and needs of each host region in terms of natural and human resources.

Clearly, humanity's Achilles' heel is our political, economic, religious, and social divisions. We should therefore move towards a more homogeneous and united world by no longer insisting on dividing factors such as tribal (national) and religious identities, but rather by emphasizing all that unites humanity, and by moving towards a planetary nation governed by a planetary body that brings all humanity together, and by sharing the Earth's resources in an equitable manner.

This means, of course, *a secular planetary government* based on an economic and social model that respects the ecology, and a global health system that can cope with the increasingly common pandemics.

This would obviously require a complete restructuring of human societies into a centralized planetary society.

The starting point for this would be the total abandonment of the tribal, or even nationalistic, mentality, followed by the gradual abolition of national states (already, in a way, underway) in favor of regional, or even continental, entities/groupings, leading eventually, perhaps within a thousand years, to a planetary nation speaking the same language and having the same common aspirations.

A frightening prospect for many of us, but at the same time inevitable and the prerequisite before we go over and colonize other planets!

The Economic Absurdity

The economic headache of mankind is related to the fact that unlike animals, that easily can find in nature what they need, we as *"incomplete beings"* are obliged to work and transform nature to achieve this. Hence, we must work to provide for our material needs, necessary for our survival. This daily struggle for survival imposes some constraints on us such as repetitive and painful tasks. Yet, labor has undergone profound transformations in both its form and its substance. The modern definition of work is an activity whose purpose is to satisfy human needs by producing something useful or by transforming nature. Precisely on this point, we distinguish ourselves from other animals of our planet. Animals, through their activity, obtain immediate satisfaction of a physiological need without it modifying the environment beyond what is necessary for their survival. We humans, on the other hand, produce beyond our needs, and our activities cause profound changes in his environment.

Today, almost most of mankind has become sedentary, living in big urban centers, and indulging themselves in a consumerism spree. Moreover, while our so-called needs largely exceed the simple requirements of our bodies, we continue inventing new ones. To this we need to add our non-material needs, namely, to feel socially useful and avoid boredom.

As for labor, we exchange the fruit of our work for a salary allowing us to satisfy our increasingly sophisticated and artificial needs. Thus, work would allow us to use our physical and intellectual capacities for our social and personal realization. In other words, by helping Man to realize his potential, work is presented as the necessary condition to reach happiness. Among other important virtues of work, one finds the possibility of creating social connection between us and society as well as offering us a recognized social place within our socio-professional group. In short, work saves us from boredom and need.

It is true that we all hate boredom, and the fact of not having a job amplifies this state. However, sometimes it seems that the disadvantages of work outweigh its supposed virtues. The reason for these negative aspects of work is probably to be found in the social organization of work.

In the beginning, primates lived in a kind of community where teamwork was the order of the day, and everyone contributed to the extent of their abilities. They lived by hunting, fishing, and gathering. As nomads, they had no fixed habitat and followed the game as it moved around.

The discovery of agriculture and the sedentarization of Man led to the emergence of *private property* which in turn completely changed human relations and their vision of the world. From then on, we witness the appearance of chiefs, wars, and inequalities. This was the beginning of dominant-dominated economic relationship, i.e., men exploiting other fellow humans.

With the introduction of animal husbandry and agriculture, production relationships evolved, starting with slavery, passing through serfdom in the feudal era and, finally, the wage-earning system of capitalism. More specifically, after the first primate communities, labor conditions deteriorated with the advent of slavery, insofar as slaves were deprived of the right of ownership over themselves and worked for free for their masters. This improved slightly in the feudal era where serfs were expected to live and work on land, owned by a lord, in exchange for personal services and royalties.

Capitalism changed this again, and while as before the power of the ruling class rested on the exploitation of the subordinate class, the latter had more freedom in comparison to the serfs, insofar as its employer held a purely professional and limited power over it.

This was because unlike communism, which gives labor the central role in the productive process, for capitalism, labor is only one commodity among many others, and only one of the elements in the chain of value creation that are labor, capital and the entrepreneur. In other words, capitalism replaced the system of lords and serfs with the single concept of *profit*, its main objective. The perpetual quest for profit was launched, which meant increasing production, reducing costs, and taking as much market share as possible. This was the beginning of a new human misery, namely *unemployment* since wages continued to fall, and manual labor was replaced by machines. This created an army of unemployed people with no purchasing power. In other words, by shifting income from labor to capital, overcapacity was created, and demand was reduced.

To solve this paradoxical situation and restore the balance between production and real purchasing power, capitalism resorted to the reduction of productive capacity by closing factories, which again led to massive unemployment.

The cyclical crises of capitalism led to the appearance of a new socio-economic paradigm, namely communism, where was aimed at a classless society where private property and wage labor would be abolished and the means of production would be pooled. In such a utopic society, work would be free of any constraint and would only have the good of the community as its goal. Yet, communism turned out to be a total failure and strengthened the position of its critics who saw it as an economic illusion.

Liberal capitalism, also known as neo-liberalism, emerged victorious from this and took advantage of this to consolidate its position. A profit machine without limits, based on fictitious capital, the growth of money supply and the creation of debt.

In an attempt to solve the problem of the opposition between overproduction and purchasing power, the neoliberals opted for the risky strategy of creating artificial demand through loans and credits. However, as expected, this turned into a fiasco and provoked an unprecedented global financial crisis in 2008.

People simply could not pay their debts, putting the global financial system on the verge of collapse. Governments stepped in to save the big banks with public money, shifting the debt from the big banks to the taxpayers who are still paying for it in the form of higher taxes and austerity measures implemented by their respective governments.

With profit as its main objective, capitalism continues to generate artificial needs that are both non-essential and ecologically harmful. The rise of e-commerce has intensified this consumerism, which continues to worsen the depletion of natural resources and pollution. We all know what happens next.

The Capitalist Dilemma

Obviously, capitalism is not a stable system and by nature, namely the perpetual search for profit through exponential growth, it contributes to the ecological collapse of the planet.

According to its critics, capitalism can hardly continue on its growth spree and its relentless pursuit of capital accumulation, which seems to have reached a quasi-standstill. Put differently, considering the limitation of our planet's natural resources, and increasing environmental problems, the perpetual capital accumulation could not go on eternally. To this we must add the impact of AI and automation, which will contribute to the gradual disappearance of the middle classes because of their impact on administrative work. According to the most pessimistic, the current process of *"disruptive-technology-led job destruction"* will come to an end in 2045 when capitalism will have disappeared!

Yet, mankind seems to be trapped in a deadlock, because capitalism, despite its cyclical crises, in the absence of a viable economic model, remains the dominant economic model. While it continues to change and adapt itself to the changing technological and social landscape, its harmful impact on our planet lingers. While not at all accountable for its effects on people and the planet, financial capitalism continues to generate poverty, inequality, and climate change.

Its main concern remains the *shareholder value*, i.e., those who hold assets and power. Hence, it continues the path of high-risk lending and other risky strategies with drastic consequences for the stock and housing markets which in turns would impact millions of people worldwide.

Even the pandemic crisis of 2020 did not change anything and many of the world's biggest companies and their shareholders enjoyed record profits during this harsh period for humanity.

Despite this daunting trend, the proponents of liberal capitalism believe that *capitalism needs to be managed, not defeated.* In other words, capitalism is diehard and still reformable so that it can metamorphose itself into a more just, inclusive, and equitable economic system.

This obviously requires a complete change of perspective, namely, to take a broader, longer-term view about the value investments create for people, for communities, and for the planet. In other words, to move towards values other than purely economic ones and to integrate a much wider circle of actors in the creation of value in companies, namely people, nature and the synergies between climate, environment and health. This would mean giving less importance to GDP and growth as indicators of wealth, since they ignore economic and social inequalities and environmental degradation.

Starting from the principle that money is not an end in itself but rather a means at the service of man, and while respecting the need to innovate and improve the performance of companies, we must encourage the creation of meaningful and fulfilling jobs, as well as incentives for a fair sharing of profits. Hence, innovation must aim at responding to societal and environmental challenges and must be directed towards local green production in large cities as well as in rural communities.

Pessimists strongly doubt the capacity and the willingness of capitalism to adapt this new value system. For them the *status que* and *business as usual* will prevail until *the point of no return*. According to the *neo-socialists*, the innate instability of capitalism has turned it into a steamroller that is gradually taking over all spheres of human existence, including the most intimate ones, our emotional lives etc. Not believing in capitalism's capacity to become more humane, they advocate for a different economic paradigm.

The Ecological Disaster

In search of a less illusory economic alternative capable of ensuring our material and environmental fulfillment, for some the answer lies in *ecology*. Originally a science of environmental protection, ecology as an economic model advocates sustainable development that while meeting the needs of present generations would not compromise the ability of future generations to do the same. Among its main objectives, we find the fight against climate change, the preservation of biodiversity and the planet's resources, solidarity, and social cohesion. According to these environmentalists, we will not be able to maintain our production and consumption patterns because infinite growth in a finite world is impossible.

They draw a dark picture of planet Earth in an alarming status at all fronts, i.e., soil, water, and air. Excessive and ill-conceived irrigation has permanently degraded the soil through accumulation of salt. Add to that water and wind erosion, chemical degradation, and physical and structural damage.

Half of the world's rivers are severely damaged or polluted. One third of the world's population is dependent on groundwater, whose level is constantly falling, leading to a chronic shortage of drinking water. More than one billion people do not have clean drinking water and more than two billion others do not have improved sanitation. This has led to the spread of water-borne diseases such as malaria, which is responsible for two million deaths every year.

Oceans are all on the verge of collapse because of oil spills, heavy metal discharges and various detritus. In addition, sedimentation, which is the result of construction activities along the coast, is seriously threatening coral reefs around the world. Moreover, one third of the world's fish stocks are in the process of being depleted due to overexploitation and overfishing.

Earth's atmosphere is also experiencing an unprecedented depletion of the ozone layer, which protects life on Earth from dangerous ultraviolet rays. And finally, the concentrations of other greenhouse gases related to the global warming phenomenon have also increased.

Massive deforestation has led to the fragmentation and disruption of habitats and wildlife. This has indirectly contributed to the appearance of deadly pandemics. Human activity such as deforestation, illegal wildlife trafficking, and air pollution has brought humans into contact with deadly viruses. These viruses have always existed all over the world in the depths of tropical forests in the organism of wild species, far from urban areas. However, by disrupting these ecosystems, we have facilitated the transmission of viruses between wild animals and humans, with farm animals representing the intermediate vector.

The ecologists claim that we have already exceeded the limits of our planet in terms of its capacity to provide the natural resources necessary for economic growth, and to assimilate the resulting waste. So, to preserve our planet we will have to put limits to growth, limit population growth, produce locally what we need, and live in voluntary simplicity. They also suggest renewable and alternative energies to replace fossil fuel. Yet, at closer inspection, one realizes these alternative energies are not that clean either.

According to the critics of the green wave, which is sweeping our planet, renewable energies will never replace fossil energies, since they cannot be stored, they are intermittent, i.e., they depend on the vagaries of nature as is the case for wind or sun. Moreover, the manufacturing of devices used in renewable energy production is also thought to be quite polluting. For example, the solar panels that are supposed to produce clean energy, are themselves made from the exploitation of quartz mines, which requires a lot of energy as well as considerable CO2 emissions.

The same goes for electrical cars, whose batteries are a major source of pollution and are quite difficult to recycle. It is to be noted that the batteries of electric cars are made of *lithium* and the factories that produce them reject a lot of waste containing uranium. This makes the production of these cars extremely polluting.

And last but not least the wind turbines, which are quite inefficient in electricity production due to their intermittent nature depending on wind, as well as their noise pollution. They are also quite difficult to recycle. If this is true, then the ecologists do not fix the problem but rather displace it.

As for degrowth recommended by ecologists, their critics consider the green model to be illusory, insofar as it ignores human nature, which is our tendency to selfishly seek to increase our well-being.

So, the only way out of this human-made mess is a complete change of paradigm and adaptation of a new lifestyle less anchored on consumerism and more respectful of nature, leading to a sustainable development of mankind. Are we at all capable of that?

The Future of Work

Nowadays, work, which is part of human rights, has become a privilege reserved for those who are better adapted and compatible with the new imperatives of the labor market. Thus, with the rise of automation and AI, a new category of people is emerging, namely *the unemployable*. More specifically, new disruptive technologies such as automation and machine learning will have a huge impact on the way we work and have made it impossible to guarantee work for everyone.

Our technological advances of the last decades and the increase of human productivity will probably allow a significant reduction of working time and the emergence of the leisure society and universal income. We can already see that more and more repetitive and boring tasks are being taken over by Artificial Intelligence and robots.

The same goes for the organization of work, which is also undergoing a transformation. We have entered an economic cycle where waged labor is destined to disappear. Gone are the days when people worked in the same company for most of their lives and even until retirement.

Henceforth, we are all condemned to change job several times during our professional lives, and we will pass from the permanent contract to more fixed-term contracts and independent work where a consultant would work for several companies at the same time and would be paid accordingly. This disappearance of the subordination relationship in favor of a give and take relationship would increase the precariousness of work.

At the same time, we must not forget that the digital era has also brought about a change in mentality, which will have enormous consequences on the corporate culture and the structure of the labor market.

On the corporate side, these changes will result in the gradual disappearance of the old hierarchical and standardized structures and their replacement by a more flexible and collaborative environment leading to more autonomy and a more fluid career path.

By examining the organization of labor since the dawn of time, one can see that the *dominant-dominated relationship* persists and that it has not changed in substance. Karl Marx refers to it by using the term *"the invisible chains"* criticizing capitalism. According to him, it is a kind of *voluntary servitude* where capitalism offers the subordinate class (modern slaves) the possibility to choose their *masters*. In other words, this consented adhesion of the employees to the productive system does not change the exploitative nature of capitalism and it imposes other constraints on them in the name of competition and profitability. Having said that one should not ignore a gradual and cumulative transformation towards better working conditions either. The question that now arises is whether the significant reduction in working time and the emergence of leisure society would finally bring about meaning and well-being at work, where workers would finally be actors in their professional lives?

The AI Challenge

Also known as the fourth industrial revolution, artificial intelligence is the bearer of many hopes and threats regarding human labor. For the pessimists, AI brings a new form of alienation at work, where humans would be replaced and dominated by these technologies, while on the other hand the optimists see AI as an ally to make our careers more interesting.

By taking care of the tedious and repetitive tasks, AI leaves us the tasks that require flexibility, agility, and creativity. Thus, it revalues our jobs by transforming them. A good example is that of a cashier's whose key skill until now have been rather technical. With the emergence of self-checkouts, this technical skill will change and become more relational.

That said, it goes without saying that robotization will inevitably lead to the disappearance of certain jobs with low added value and often less rewarding. These include cleaning ladies, assistants, canteen staff and workers in the mining, construction, and transport industries. To that one must also add some white-collar jobs such as bank and insurance employees, accounting employees and executive secretaries. At the same time, we must not forget that there are still many industries and tasks that are not made for a robot. The list is long: care takers, housekeepers, nurses, speech therapists, psychologists, chiropodists, pharmacists, etc. However, one can also argue that the assumption according to which humans are indispensable in certain fields of activity could prove illusory. In other words, as times goes by, more and more tasks will be entrusted to AI. Not only those of the economic life like medicine, education, and law, but also those on the fringe of the economic life. Philosophical chatbots are an example with which we could address our existential questions!

The other big challenge imposed on us by the emergence of AI would be its impact on globalization and international division of labor. In other words, AI will most probably disrupt the current paradigm of international division of labor, whereby, the low-income countries take charge of most labor-intensive parts of the value chain.

More specifically, the current trend of regionalization of supply chains, triggered by the Covid-19 pandemic, would prompt companies to relocate their activities to favor national and regional supply chains. This is now possible thanks to technological advances in the fields of robotics, artificial intelligence and 3D printing, which allow rapid delivery of increasingly personalized products.

Put differently, these new technologies, in a way, have removed the comparative advantages of low-income countries and allow automated manufacturing together with its associated services and processes, to be carried out, at a lower cost by robots and AI.

So, why not do it in the basement of a head office in Europe, rather than moving the production to the other side of the planet.

A quite reassuring prospect for the Western world, but less encouraging for low-income countries with a young population of job seekers. Having said that the West will not escape this fate either and there will be generally fewer activities left to be done by humans.

This will render the implementation of *the universal basic income* indispensable. This is an income established for all citizens of a country from the age of majority to death. This income would consist of a monthly citizen's salary without any conditions, which can be cumulative with other incomes. Thus, people would have the choice to work to earn more.

As for the financing of this project, the developed countries could eventually do it by taxing their high-tech and robotic companies. This would be more difficult for overpopulated and low-income countries, hence humanity's obligation to universalize this project in order to fight inequality and ensure world peace.

By all accounts, the merger of information technology and biotech will drive billions out of the labor market and in the longer run, human labor will become obsolete. Consequently, the challenge of governments would not be to create jobs but rather to pay (universal income) and keep an army of unemployable people busy with leisure activities.

Already now, work and leisure constitute the two central activities in our lives. Put differently, our social lives seem to alternate between work and leisure in a percentage that varies according to time, age and country. Moreover, thanks to the productivity gains made possible by our technological advances, we have been witnessing a constant reduction in working hours for several decades, and there are even those who anticipate the gradual end of human work. This decrease in working hours combined with the increase in life expectancy will inevitably lead to the emergence of a leisure society. A society that focuses its economy on all the leisure services that can be offered to citizens. In other words, after religion and industry the new structuring element of society will be leisure. At first look this new emerging leisure society sounds tempting, but at closer inspections things are not that shiny either.

Leisure has also turned into a powerful means of controlling and manipulating the masses. While for a long-time force and repression were the main strategies of dictators, the free world, namely the West, immediately saw the usefulness of futile and hedonistic pleasures as an antidepressant of the masses. Also known as *Huxley's dystopia*, in such a society unrestrained pleasures and non-stimulating entertainments are the pillars of mass entertainment, promoting *self-distraction and dissociated happiness.*

Authoritarian regimes, faced with the ineffectiveness of *Orwellian repression,* which often leads to rebellion, have also begun to adopt a hybrid approach (*Huxley-Orwell*) based on technoscience. More precisely, this consists, on the one hand of occupying their citizens with futile hobbies and on the other hand, of monitoring them by mobile applications and video surveillance everywhere. This hybrid model of mass control seems to work, at least for now.

The proponents of this approach are convinced that by building a civilization of futile and hedonistic pleasures the masses can be controlled forever.

Markets and dictators aside, the confluence of productivity gains, robotization, and the expansion of the use of AI in all branches of the economy would inevitably lead to the emergence of a new leisure society. In such a society, labor and leisure would belong to consumption, independent of each other.

Finally, thanks to our advances in all fields, we are finally able to follow the advice of Blaise Pascal who encouraged us to distract ourselves from the "essential" by resorting to entertainment. By the way, in Pascal's time, entertainment was a privilege of the rich, to which the working classes had little access.

Entertainment offers us a solution to avoid facing the tragic nature of existence. Thus, by filling our free time, entertainment helps us to empty our heads instead of filling them with existential questions that lead us nowhere and that often give way only when we no longer try to solve them. However, this praise of entertainment often clashes with the arguments of its opponents who criticize its standardized and impersonal vision. Basically, according to them, as prisoners of work, we are forced to work more and more, which has transformed leisure into a kind of *dolce vita*. But the delights of consumption that offer us entertainment are only ephemeral satisfactions, condemning us to constant oscillation between boredom and suffering.

The critics of modern leisure remind us of its downside, namely the race towards the material means of distraction. In other words, after the frenzy of accumulation of material goods generated by capitalism, the latter pushes us into a new frantic race for personal fulfillment, triggered by a growing desire for distraction. And if we fail to satisfy this desire, which is often the case, we end up frustrated and feeling *poor*. What about a complete change of perspective, where we try to approach the subject of *work-leisure* from a completely different angle? Maybe our thirst for distraction comes from the fact that our jobs are not fulfilling. What if we tried to improve the less fulfilling jobs, by making them more interesting? After all, the ability of work to be fulfilling depends on the amount of *fun* or *sense* that it contains.

In any case, the rise of AI and the robotization of tedious and repetitive tasks will relieve humans of tedious jobs. This tendency will also accelerate the *scarcity* of work, which in turn will inevitably devoid the latter from its existential virtues and give the baton to leisure, as the main source of personal fulfillment.

Unlike culture, which can be divisive, entertainment has this unique ability to bring people together. However, we must not forget that intuitively, unlimited entertainment will be boring. Moreover, immersive virtual worlds, cleverly designed to tap into our core emotions, are becoming more and more addictive. So, what is the solution?

The transhumanists might hold the answer this dilemma. They refer to the so-called biology of boredom, where via genetic manipulations we would be able to transform human nature. In other words, biotechnologies will improve our hedonic range, by diversifying our palette of emotions and by eradicating the molecular substrates of boredom in favor of those of fascination.

Thus, by making boredom physiologically impossible, this biological revolution will mark a major evolutionary transition for humanity. The end of the alternation between wage slavery and empty hedonism and the beginning of a fulfilling post-Darwinian life. Let's hope it will come true one day!

In the meantime, while waiting for the transhumanist utopia, the notion of leisure remains a dimension of Man with which we have an ambivalent relationship. On the one hand, the drama of boredom and solitude pushes un into the uncertainty of entertainment, but at the same time, the latter remains the best resort against the weight of existence.

It is likely that the prospect of a generalized universal income, associated with an unlimited abundance of material goods, will lead to the reduction of poverty and an important increase of our free time. Thus, the new challenge of mankind would be to keep busy and to entertain us in an intelligent and fulfilling way.

The Cyclical Absurdity

After having reviewed the different manifestations of the absurd, it would seem that we are subject to a universal principle called *the transcendental dialectics*. The universe and all its contents seem to oscillate perpetually between two extremities of a cycle.

The cycle of *"big crunch-big bang"* at universal level, as well as the cycle of day and night and that of the seasons at terrestrial level, are examples of this. Yet a closer inspection reveals that it is more of a *spiral* rather than a circle. A bit like the image of galaxies, namely a curve that rotates around an axis and which forms a winding in space. A circle or a cycle, by nature being repetitive means immobility, while a spiral introduces an additional dimension, i.e., movement and evolution.

Both axial and evolutionary, spiral represents permanence within change, or if you will, permanence disguised in movement. This circular movement of the spiral, extended to infinity, leads to a movement of creation that is constantly renewed.

It is thus a question of balance in imbalance, inducing the notion of cycle and recommencement. This indicates that *everything that happens has already happened and will happen again but in a more evolved form.*

The dominant-dominated relationship is a good example of this, insofar as it still persists but has changed in form without changing in substance.

On the political level, such an evolution can be seen in the passage from dictatorship to democracy where domination by constraint has been replaced by a system of domination by freedom, desire, and consent. The same observation on the economic level would be the replacement of slavery by voluntary servitude in capitalism where one has the possibility to choose one's master. In other words, the power of the dominant class over the subordinate class persists, but it has changed form and modern workers have more freedom than slaves and serfs.

The same trend applies to the history of paradigms, where one observes a dynamic process in which each paradigm brings with it a small portion of reality.

This means that there are some parts of truth in all previous paradigms and the dialectics through a mechanism of conservation and overcoming has been able to eliminate the errors and dogmatisms of these systems in a continuous and cumulative way.

We can even compare this cumulative process to a nuclear fusion where several atomic nuclei (theories) unite to form a single heavier nucleus (a step closer to the truth), and a great quantity of energy (the engine of history). Thus, the criticism of the previous paradigms was necessary in order to perfect them. This tendency of the paradigms to believe that they are always at the end of everything that precedes them, has always proved to be false and illusory.

The force behind this perpetual autodynamics is most probably the *transcendental dialectics,* according to which everything that exists passes through its opposite, which is the force behind all evolution.

A good example of this doctrine would be death, which in some way is the condition for the recommencement and the generational cycle. Thus, life nourishes death and vice versa.

The Universe is in a constant state of flux and change and movement. While these infinite changes are most often slow and gradual, they are often marked by sudden and abrupt movements that metamorphose the situation and state of things completely.

Based on the Spinozian causality, i.e., everything arises from something with relation to what existed before, these sudden evolutions are in some way the qualitative outcome of a quantitative process.

It seems that we are trapped in a universe which is subjected to the laws of dialectics grasping everything from its birth, its movement, and development up to its end. An end which is not a pure disappearance, but an overcoming, which is at the same time negation and conservation. The *end* in the dialectical sense does not mean finitude but rather the beginning of the destruction of established norms. It is a perpetual cycle of the conversion of potential into realization.

As the quintessence of polarization, dialectic seeks truth at the other end of the extreme. Nevertheless, the relativism that could result from this should not lead us to apathy, but rather to realistic pragmatism.

Yet, one could ask rightfully, what is the point in a universe which oscillates between expansion and contraction, and a life swinging between boredom and suffering, while waiting for death, a *Sisyphean condemnation!*

Epilogue

An absurd universe gave birth to *Absurdistan*, our beloved planet Earth, which obviously bears the same heritage, i.e., devoid of any sense. This explains the complexity of the human condition, i.e., our exhausting quest for a purpose in life. The legitimate question is whether we will ever get there? In other words, in a world so relative, subjective, and uncertain, aren't we all doomed to doubt or illusion?

At least for now, the real world seems to be beyond our reach and the elusive bottom of reality escapes our capacities of comprehension, which makes it unattainable. This existential powerlessness amplifies the feeling of absurdity.

Faced with the tragic nature of human existence, many of us prefer to escape the bitter reality of our lives, taking refuge in a less tragic version of existence. However, despite the comforting character of this defensive mechanism, which is the escape from reality, it often proves ineffective, and instead sinks us in neurosis and confusion.

Don Quixote's answer to the absurdity of life was *denial* and taking refuge in *madness*, while Sisyphus kept on fighting a *perpetual* and *desperate battle*. Faced with this existential impasse, the only two possible solutions would be *suicide* or *faith*.

Obviously, the great leap into the irrational, which is faith, seems to be the easiest and even quickest solution for relieving our existential anguishes. After all, despite its illusory nature and its impertinence in the modern world, the reassurance that faith provides does the trick for many of us. However, often by cultivating guilt and turning us away from life, religion poisons our lives. Thus, faith according to Albert Camus would be *a philosophical, and intellectual suicide.*

As for physical suicide, this *sublime courage of the defeated,* in the face of the elusive feeling of absurdity, might seem tempting. It will allow us to escape from a tragic existence, but if we look at it more closely, it will not make sense at all. According to Camus, by ending one's life, existence would become more absurd. Instead, he advocates a defiant refusal of the absurd. More precisely, while recognizing the absurdity of existence, one must transform it into something as pleasant as possible.

This brings us to a *third option,* which consists of a *quasi-cynical* and yet *lucid approach to existence,* i.e., to expose the reality of life as it is. This might lead to anxiety at first, what they call the *vertigo of freedom.*

This exercise of unveiling the real nature of existence requires equally *a great yes* to life, to the good as well as the evil, to our successes as well as our failures.

By recognizing the tragic nature of life, we should *embrace it and love life without expecting it to love us back.*

In the same vein, life should not be seen as a problem to be solved, but rather as a reality to be lived. Our desire to take refuge in *the elegance and perfection of the ideal* and to flee from reality is the very source of our suffering and disappointment.

This lucid approach to the human condition does not mean blindly loving one's destiny and thus accepting one's fate, but rather transfiguring it by an active *"Amor Fati"* approach. In other words, to look at the full half of the glass and in the face of suffering to say: *"I suffer, therefore I exist"* and to look at death with a tranquil gaze and consider it as a total deprivation of any possibility of suffering. After all, it is death that makes life precious and thanks to which we can continue to exist.

By excluding any reference to the future, we could stand up to the trials of life. This absence of hope is one of the conditions of authentic joy, a paradoxical joy, since it springs from the very heart of everything that hinders it. In other words, a kind of acute pleasure, namely the *happiness of a glorious suffering*!

So, which approach to choose? There is no standard solution, and everyone is supposed to find his/her own way. Nevertheless, there are a few facts to consider, no matter what we choose.

Firstly, it is better to accept our limitations, that is, the fact that as *limited* beings we do not have much control over anything. Obviously, we are in an infinite universe, cold and quite indifferent to us. Our planet is not the center of the Universe, and we are only a beast among other animals. Additionally, we are also subject to the tyranny of the unconscious and our innate drives.

Secondly, we should embark on an exercise of self-knowledge and overcoming fear, to open ourselves to reality. According to all evidence, we are full of paradoxes and the only way of freeing ourselves from them is to become aware of them. To understand that *dissatisfaction* is the mark of our condition, and that we are our own worst enemy.

We have contradictory needs to *admire* and to *possess* and then to turn away from it when we have achieved it. So, the first step involves the recognition of all our flaws and shortcomings.

Third, we would be better off if we simply stopped projecting our way of thinking onto the world, which is neither organized nor static. The world is random, volatile, complex, and perfectly interconnected, which often results in unexpected and unpleasant feedback to us, which frustrates us even more. Once we admit that the world is complex, organic, and intertwined with a pinch of *randomness*, things will become more bearable for all of us.

Fourth, let us abandon our *Manichean* approach to the world that takes us from one extreme to the other, often while seeking to overcompensate for a previous mistake. Democracy and sexual liberation are good examples of this, as we have gone through both extremes before we got to some sort of equilibrium. So today, our attitude towards sexuality lies somewhere between the *Victorian repression* and the *libertinism* of the sixties. Hence, a more nuanced approach to the world around us could perhaps prevent us from getting lost between the extremes.

Fifth, everything in the Universe is subject to the laws of *transcendental dialectics*, namely evolution and forward movement. In other words, the world consists of opposite but not necessarily opposing ideas or concepts which, when put together, either negate each other or synthesise into a new *whole*. In the same way the latter generates its opposite and leads to a new synthesis, and so on ad infinitum. Consequently, it is imperative that we change fundamentally and accept that nothing is eternal, and that whatever we do, change will come.

Faced with this *dialectical determinism*, namely permanent movement, and evolution, we are better off not fearing it and instead embracing it. Yet, on a personal level, this adaptation to new situations can be achieved by constantly questioning and reinventing ourselves, which sometimes can also be quite exhausting.

That said, moving forward does not always mean progress in the right sense of the word. This ambiguity of progress is manifested in its capacity to be both emancipating and alienating. In fact, progress is never linear and can be a bumpy ride. In other words, a gradual and cumulative transformation towards the better, while passing through "cut-off" periods as was the case in the Dark Middle Ages. However, adaptation to change does not mean fatalism or submission. The renaissance is a good example of this, where Man succeeded in replacing religious dogma with reason and human creativity.

By applying the same principle to our current technological frenzy, we would obviously need *a second renaissance*. While bringing us countless benefits, technology has replaced religion and is currently dominating our personal and professional lives. A digital dictatorship, or rather an algorithmic society, where we are permanently controlled in everything we do, namely the way we communicate, search, buy, entertain, and learn.

Therefore, by taking inspiration from the first renaissance, we need to replace *technological dogma* with *human relevance*. Our evaluation criteria in this endeavor should simply be the degree to which technology makes us more *human*. It is time to break the *technological tyranny* and aim for authenticity, engagement, quality relationships and personal and collective fulfillment.

Sixth, perhaps it is time to stop spinning our brains out and simply abandoning the futile search for absolute happiness which is out of our reach. It is therefore better to adopt the lucidity that will lead us to the *"tragic joy"*, i.e., the capacity to accept existence, despite its tragic character. This would consist in abstaining from existential anguish and going towards all the present enjoyments, without worrying about the past or the future. Let's ignore completely the existential questionings, which only give way when we don't try to solve them anymore.

And last but not least, let's make the most of the time that we have left in *the limbo of the living*!

Index

ABSURDISTAN